THE 1,000 YEAR REIGN OF JESUS CHRIST ON THE EARTH

THE 1,000 YEAR REIGN OF JESUS CHRIST ON THE EARTH

WILL YOU MAKE IT or MISS IT?

Dale M. Sides

The scriptures used throughout this study are quoted from the King James Version unless otherwise noted. Any explanatory insertions by the author within a scripture are enclosed in brackets [ ]. Any words in boldface within a verse indicate the author's emphasis.

THE 1,000 YEAR REIGN OF JESUS CHRIST ON THE EARTH
©2006 by Liberating Publications, Inc.
ISBN 1-930433-22-0

Published by:
Liberating Publications, Inc.
PO Box 974
Bedford, VA 24523
www.liberatingpublications.com

All rights reserved. Published 2006
Printed in the United States of America

No part of this book may be reproduced or transmitted in any form or by any means, electronic or mechanical, including photocopying, recording, or by any information storage and retrieval system, without permission in writing from the publisher.

To my four daughters:
Sarah, Jessica, Hannah, and Elisabeth.
Thank you for willingly and graciously sharing
my life with this pursuit of the inheritance
of the millennial kingdom.

Contents

Introduction	1
Section One—The Kingdom Explained	7
Chapter 1—The Two Gospels	9
Chapter 2—The Kingdom Lost	19
Chapter 3—The Outline of the Ages	26
Chapter 4—Understanding the End-Time Sequence of Events	34
Chapter 5—The Sufferings and the Glory of the Lord	41
Section Two—Understanding Our Inheritances	51
Chapter 6—The Inheritances of Grace and Reward	53
Chapter 7—The Bride Comes Out of the Body	62
Chapter 8—Reigning with the Lord	71
Section Three—Entering the Kingdom	77
Chapter 9—The Judgment Seat of Christ	79
Chapter 10—The Out Resurrection	86
Chapter 11—The Good and Faithful Servant	93
Chapter 12—Laboring to Enter into the Rest	99
Chapter 13—Keys to Entering the Kingdom	105
Section Four—Missing the Kingdom	117
Chapter 14—Seeing the Kingdom but Not Entering It	119
Chapter 15—The Outer Darkness	122
Chapter 16—Gehenna	133
Chapter 17—The Close of the Kingdom	143
Conclusion	151

Appendixes 153
    Appendix A—The Woman Who Hid
        the Kingdom 155
    Appendix B—The Kingdom of God and
        the Kingdom of Heaven 174
    Appendix C—Can You Lose Your Salvation? ... 183
    Appendix D—Life in the Millennial Kingdom ... 187
    Appendix E—Rewards in the Kingdom
        of the Father 189
    Appendix F—The Word "Eternal" 193
    Appendix G—Matthew 24:14 197

Notes 201

Index 205

INTRODUCTION

The Bible clearly testifies that a 1,000-year reign of Jesus is scheduled to occur on the earth. Since the degree of accuracy for biblical prophecy is so high that it is almost mathematically impossible to describe, it behooves every man, woman, and child on the earth to heed this advanced notice and to prepare for this coming kingdom. You can be included, or you can miss it. Admittance is availed to each and every person by God's grace, but every candidate must prove him- or herself worthy for this kingdom. Rest assured, it *is* coming, whether you are ready or not.

For many years my theology did not even contain a cubicle into which I could file this doctrine. The extent of my understanding concerning the future was that if I believed in Jesus then I would go to heaven, either after I died or at the rapture of the church. I thank the Lord for that much understanding and I still believe that, but before the new heavens and earth are going to be made, there will be a 1,000-year kingdom coming to this earth.

> *Blessed and holy is he that hath part in the first resurrection: on such the second death hath no power, but they shall be priests of God and of Christ, and shall reign with him a thousand years.*   Revelation 20:6

This biblical truth has been buried and hidden out of sight from Christianity since about A.D. 350, but now the Holy Spirit is endeavoring to restore this truth into prominence, because knowledge of how to enter this kingdom will fuel commitment within Christians like no other subject in the Bible. It did it for the early church, and it will do it for the church of these last days, too. The Roman emperor Constantine (along with the theologian Augustine) hid this truth by not teaching about this period of time and stating that it was allegorical, and not a literal truth. This was an assault on the kingdom of Christ—an attempt to negate and deny the prophecy that a future kingdom would come and crush all other kingdoms. It is time to get out our shovels and dig this gem up from the rubble of confusion and deception, and let the whole Word of God be known about the prophetic promises that will be imparted to those who are faithful in serving the Lord. This is the incentive the Holy Spirit is seeking to give His people—to keep them motivated during this time of harvest and apostasy.

This truth about the 1,000-year reign of Jesus on the earth is called the "gospel of the kingdom," and it is the next step beyond the gospel of grace—so abundantly known and taught. Jesus and John preached this gospel of the kingdom and passed it on to the apostles and prophets of the early church. This was the mainstay of the early church and the impetus that moved Christianity faster during that time than in any other in the history of the church. It is the good news (gospel) of the 1,000-year reign of Christ on the earth that

Introduction

will include those individuals who are committed to the cause of Christ, which is building God's kingdom on the earth.

This is indeed good news! During this 1,000-year period on the earth, Satan will be chained (Revelation 20:1–3). This will be life on the earth the way God has always planned it. It will be "Thy kingdom has come," and "Thy will (will) be done on earth as it is in heaven," because Jesus will be here as King to make it so. Jesus will live and reign as King of the world from Jerusalem; King David will be king over the Jews (Ezekiel 34:23–24); the 12 apostles will rule over the 12 tribes of Israel (Matthew 19:28); and Jesus' faithful disciples will rule over the cities and towns around the world (Luke 19:17–19). This will be life on a devil-free planet! It will be Satan-free (Revelation 20:1–4), poverty-free (Psalm 72:2), war-free (Isaiah 2:4), sickness-free (Isaiah 35:5–6) and hunger-free (Amos 9:13). It will be a mosquito-free, ant-free picnicking paradise.

As exciting as this truth is, and as good as the news is that you can make this kingdom, the other side of the coin is that you can miss it, too.

> *But the children of the kingdom shall be cast out into outer darkness: there shall be weeping and gnashing of teeth.*   Matthew 8:12

All Christians have been given eternal life by the grace of God—the right to live in the new heavens and earth (Revelation 21:7). Access into the millennial kingdom, however, will be granted only to those who have labored in service for Christ during their life on earth. There will be many Christians who will view this kingdom from the outer darkness (Matthew 22:13–14). They will weep due to their sorrow of not participating in it. They will gnash their teeth in anger, either for not knowing about it so they could have been in on it, or for not living according to the standards required to qualify for it.

THE 1,000 YEAR REIGN OF JESUS CHRIST ON THE EARTH

Every Christian will go to the judgment seat of Christ and will hear either:

> *Well done, thou good and faithful servant: thou hast been faithful over a few things, I will make thee ruler over many things: enter thou into the joy of thy lord.*   *Matthew 25:21*

OR . . .

> *Thou wicked and slothful servant . . . cast ye the unprofitable servant into outer darkness: there shall be weeping and gnashing of teeth.*
>   *Matthew 25:26a, 30*

There is a 1,000-year reign of Jesus Christ coming to the earth. Will you make it or miss it? It is the Father's good pleasure to give you the kingdom.

> *Fear not, little flock; for it is your Father's good pleasure to give you the kingdom.*
>   *Luke 12:32*

Yes, it is the Father's will for you to be in that kingdom; but be not deceived—what you sow is what you will reap (Galatians 6:7). The Father will give to each man his rightful due, for He is no respecter of persons.

> *And if ye call on the Father, who without respect of persons judgeth according to every man's work, pass the time of your sojourning here in fear.*   *1 Peter 1:17*

> *And whatsoever ye do, do it heartily, as to the Lord, and not unto men; knowing that of the Lord ye shall receive the reward of the inheritance: for ye serve the Lord Christ. But he that doeth wrong shall receive for the wrong which he hath done: and there is no respect of persons.*   *Colossians 3:23–25*

Introduction

The purpose of this book is to motivate you to strive for the masteries and to show you how to enter this kingdom. Our study is laced with the promise of being in the kingdom and yet it also contains the fear (of the Lord) of missing it, too. Be well assured that this kingdom is coming to the earth and will exist, either with us or without us. There is a 1,000-year reign of Jesus coming to the earth. Will you make it, or will you miss it? What you do *today* determines the answer to that question.

SECTION ONE
THE KINGDOM EXPLAINED

The content of the first five chapters of this book will lay a foundational understanding of the kingdom of heaven. As with all structures, if the foundation is solid and straight, the building can stand. We must patiently dig our way out from beneath the rubble of confusion collected over the past 2,000 years, so we need to be certain that we develop a sound understanding. Since the 1,000-year reign with Jesus Christ on this earth is at stake, we must go slowly enough to make sure that every building block is in place.

These chapters will explain what the gospel of the kingdom is, how the gospel of the kingdom was lost, and that it will actually exist here on this earth. A complete picture of the ages (including past, present, and future) will be provided so that we can determine our position now and know what to expect in the future.

All of this detailed information is necessary in order to achieve our objective of learning how to enter this promised kingdom, and it will be exciting to uncover these great gems of truth, just as digging in an archeological site offers potential insight at the turning of each stone. We must be patient to understand these things and forgiving of our Christian ancestors, knowing that they did not intentionally allow these treasures to be stolen, but they were victims of the plans and ploys of Satan. Once these truths are regained, we will be able to have the same momentum of evangelism the early church had, with their same measure of commitment, knowing that we are vying for entrance into the Lord's promised kingdom.

CHAPTER 1
THE TWO GOSPELS

Much confusion about the coming reign of Jesus on the earth has arisen because of a lack of understanding about the term "gospel." Many assume that because they have heard the good news about salvation and eternal life that they have heard the whole truth. As precious as this particular truth is, it is only part of a much bigger picture. We all need to hear "the truth, the whole truth, and nothing else but the truth." (And may we add, "This we will do—so help us, God.")

Allow me to address a reservation you may be dealing with right now. In Galatians 1 Paul says,

> *But even if we, or an angel from heaven, preach any other gospel to you than what we have preached to you, let him be accursed. As we have said before, so now I say again, if anyone preaches any other gospel to you than what you have received, let him be accursed.*
> *Galatians 1:8–9 NKJ*

While we certainly do not want to bring any curse upon ourselves by promoting "another gospel," we also do not intend to allow a vital truth that was originally taught as an integral part of the gospel of Christ to continue to lie in ruins amidst the rubble of neglect.

Peter, one of Jesus' chief apostles, exhorted the early church to be good stewards of the manifold (meaning complex, variegated, and intricate) grace of God.

> *As every man hath received the gift, even so minister the same one to another, as good stewards of the manifold grace of God.*
> *1 Peter 4:10*

This responsibility for stewardship was also addressed by Paul in his letters.

> *Let a man so account of us, as of the ministers of Christ, and stewards of the mysteries of God. Moreover it is required in stewards, that a man be found faithful.*
> *1 Corinthians 4:1*

Good stewardship involves faithfulness. We must be found faithful in preserving the mysteries of God. The word "mysteries" is in the plural. While there are certainly many tremendous mysteries contained within the whole truth of the gospel that we do know and hold dear, we cannot afford to deny the possibility that we may be ignorant of a key concept. We are not preaching "another gospel" by stating that anything or anyone else is needed to complete the redemptive work God sent Jesus to accomplish. From the cross on Calvary, Jesus Christ said, "It is finished." His witness is true. He lived a sinless life and died a horribly painful death to make the full gospel available to everyone. We simply want to recapture an obscured but vital aspect of this full gospel He entrusted to His stewards on earth.

To discover the whole truth we find there are two aspects of the gospel. The word "gospel" means "good news." It is the Greek word *euaggellos* and is composed of *eu* (good) and *aggello* (to announce). So, as exciting as it is to hear the good news of Jesus' coming and giving life to all those who believe in Him, there is also the good news that He is coming again and will give life to all those who are committed to live for Him. The first good news is called "the gospel of grace" and the second is called "the gospel of the kingdom."

The gospel of grace is the good news that God the Father sent His Son Jesus Christ to die for us, and to redeem us from death and give us eternal life. This is unequivocally true and can never be denied, and it is upon this primary foundation that we must now build our understanding of Jesus' coming 1,000-year reign and the gospel of the kingdom.

Imagine a courier racing across the plains as fast as he could go, with his horse's hooves pounding the prairie to reach your settlement as quickly as possible. He dismounts from his horse, smiles widely at you, and opens the dispatch. You read the good news that a fort has been built and that you can now be protected from the perils of frontier living. As you and your family dance around in excitement, you see another courier coming over the horizon. He likewise races toward you, and as he dismounts from his horse and hands you the dispatch, he also breaks into a big grin. You read the second part of the good news: You have been given land and a home within the fort, because of your faithful work to settle the frontier.

We have received the good news of eternal life and perhaps we ask ourselves, "Could this get any better?" Yes, it can, because the other good news is that before the new heavens and earth begin, a 1,000-year period of time is coming upon the earth for those who have faithfully served the Lord. This does not negate the good news of the eventual creation of the new heavens and earth; it is additional good news that precedes it (chronologically).

Look at these two verses of scripture and see the two gospels—the double blessing of the Lord.

> *But none of these things move me, neither count I my life dear unto myself, so that I might finish my course with joy, and the ministry, which I have received of the Lord Jesus, to testify the gospel of the grace of God.*
> Acts 20:24

> *And Jesus went about all the cities and villages, teaching in their synagogues, and preaching the gospel of the kingdom, and healing every sickness and every disease among the people.* Matthew 9:35

Not knowing about the gospel of the kingdom (the good news of the coming reign of Jesus on the earth) has left us with only one option of hope—to look for the new heavens and earth. But there is more good news, and both Jesus and John the Baptist preached it: The coming kingdom is at hand.

> *In those days came John the Baptist, preaching in the wilderness of Judaea, And saying, Repent ye: for the kingdom of heaven is at hand.* Matthew 3:1–2

These gospels complement each other and are in no way contradictory. The gospel of grace is fundamental and the gospel of the kingdom builds upon it. They are like twin branches of a giant oak tree of hope and stability for every Christian. The good news of grace is the guarantee of promise with the Father, and the good news of the kingdom is that a time with the Son is available, too.

Even though our focus is on the gospel of the kingdom and the 1,000-year reign with Jesus on the earth, the gospel of grace needs to be specifically discussed in order to fully grasp the sure foundation of the gospel of the kingdom.

The Gospel of Grace

"Grace" is the Greek word *charis* and means "a favor or goodness bestowed upon someone." Grace is just that; it is a gift of God's goodness given to us based upon His giving, not our works or worthiness to earn it.

> *For by grace are ye saved through faith; and that not of yourselves: it is the gift of God.*
> *Ephesians 2:8*

> *Being justified freely by his grace through the redemption that is in Christ Jesus.*
> *Romans 3:24*

This gospel of grace is God's free gift of eternal life to you.

> *That being justified by his grace, we should be made heirs according to the hope of eternal life.*
> *Titus 3:7*

> *That as sin hath reigned unto death, even so might grace reign through righteousness unto eternal life by Jesus Christ our Lord.*
> *Romans 5:21*

"To be born again" is how the Word of God describes this truth of the gospel of grace. When people accept Jesus Christ as their Savior and Lord, they are born of the Spirit (John 3:3). At that time, they are born as citizens into the kingdom of God. It is by the grace of God that they are born into this kingdom.

> *Giving thanks unto the Father, which hath made us meet to be partakers of the inheritance of the saints in light: Who hath delivered us from the power of darkness, and hath translated us [made us to become citizens] into the kingdom of his dear Son.*
> *Colossians 1:12–13*

The 1,000 Year Reign of Jesus Christ on the Earth

The kingdom is also born within us at that time, and the Holy Spirit begins working within us to bring it to pass on earth.

> *Neither shall they say, Lo here! or, lo there! for, behold, the kingdom of God is within you.*
> *Luke 17:21*

Yes, the kingdom is born within all Christians by the grace of God, but it must be worked out as we labor to build it here on the earth. That is why Jesus taught us to pray, "Thy kingdom come; Thy will be done on earth as it is in heaven." The kingdom is alive on the planet now because it was birthed within the gospel of grace. All disciples who strive for the masteries (2 Timothy 2:5) are bringing the kingdom to pass on the earth. In that sense, the kingdom is already here on the earth, but in a greater sense, it will come into full fruition when the King comes again to the earth.

We do look for the 1,000-year reign to begin later, but even now we are working to build God's kingdom on the earth. This 1,000-year reign is still going to come to pass; it will be realized when Jesus returns to the earth, and it will be given to those individuals who labor to build the kingdom now. This initial hope begins with the new birth of the gospel of grace. After the millennial kingdom, the final details of the gospel of grace will unfold when God reveals the new heavens and earth, which have been prepared for all those who believe.

> *And I saw a new heaven and a new earth: for the first [former] heaven and the first [former] earth were passed away; and there was no more sea.*
> *Revelation 21:1*

This promise is an inheritance of grace that will be given to us by God at the end of the age of the present heavens and earth.

> *Nevertheless we, according to his promise, look for new heavens and a new earth, wherein dwelleth righteousness.*   *2 Peter 3:13*

We are going to find that before this inheritance of grace is granted, there exists an inheritance of merit given to those who faithfully serve the Lord. This is the additional good news which in no way contradicts the gospel of grace. We will discover that one inheritance is given by the Father and the other is given by the Son.

The Gospel of the Kingdom

The good news of the gospel of the kingdom concerns the millennial (1,000-year) reign of Jesus on the earth. It was prophesied long before Jesus set foot on the earth.

> *And in the days of these kings shall the God of heaven set up a kingdom, which shall never be destroyed: and the kingdom shall not be left to other people, but it shall break in pieces and consume all these kingdoms, and it shall stand for ever.*   *Daniel 2:44*

When John the Baptist came, he began to announce this good news (Matthew 3:1–2). He called it the kingdom of heaven or, in other words, the reign of the King from heaven.

> *In those days came John the Baptist, preaching in the wilderness of Judaea, And saying, Repent ye: for the kingdom of heaven is at hand.*   *Matthew 3:1–2*

Jesus preached it too, and why not? He was (and still is) that King from heaven.

> *From that time Jesus began to preach, and to say, Repent: for the kingdom of heaven is at hand.*   *Matthew 4:17*

There are many, many documentations of this gospel. Matthew 4:23, 9:35, and 24:14 call it specifically by name: the gospel of the kingdom. There are 33 usages of this phrase in the book of Matthew alone. It is also referred to as "the salvation of the soul," whereas the gospel of grace is "the salvation of the spirit." This gospel of the kingdom is so well documented that when it is finally spelled out, it actually becomes a little embarrassing to see that it has always been right there in the Bible, and many of us have simply read over it or passed it by.

One of the easiest ways of distinguishing these two gospels is by looking at the usages of "the gospel of God" and "the gospel of Christ." The gospel of grace is also called the gospel of God, and the gospel of the kingdom is also called the gospel of Christ. When we examine these usages, it verifies without a doubt that there are two gospels and that each has its own inheritance and stipulations for obedience.

The Gospel of God

There are seven usages of the phrase "the gospel of God" in the Word of God.[1] All seven emphasize the gift of God's grace and are the documentation in the Pauline epistles of this inheritance of grace and its guarantee of the new heavens and earth. Here are a few of them with explanatory notes to show the difference.

> *That I should be the minister of Jesus Christ to the Gentiles, ministering the gospel of God [grace is used in verse 15], that the offering up of the Gentiles [who were purchased by the blood of Jesus] might be acceptable, being sanctified by the Holy Ghost.   Romans 15:16*
>
> *For the time is come that judgment must begin at the house of God: and if it first begin at us [who are saved], what shall the end be of them that obey not the gospel of God [given by grace]?   1 Peter 4:17*

All of these usages emphasize the grace given by believing on Jesus Christ, with no strings attached or works required.

The Gospel of Christ

There are 11 usages of the phrase "the gospel of Christ."[2] These also are the documentation in the Pauline epistles of this gospel of the kingdom. Notice in the examples chosen that the emphasis given in these verses demonstrates the need for obedience; this gospel is not received by grace alone.

> *Whiles by the experiment of this ministration [service] they glorify God for your professed subjection [by obedience] unto the gospel of Christ, and for your liberal distribution unto them, and unto all men.*   2 Corinthians 9:13

> *Only let your conduct be worthy [through obedience] of the gospel of Christ, so that whether I come and see you or am absent, I may hear of your affairs, that you stand fast in one spirit, with one mind striving together [by works] for the faith of the gospel.*
>   Philippians 1:27 NKJ

These two gospels are strongly emphasized throughout the New Testament. The gospel of grace is the gospel of God; it is the foundation of the new birth. It is given by grace, not by works. It cannot be lost, and is the gift of eternal life.

The gospel of the kingdom is the gospel of Christ, and this gospel emphasizes the need for obedience once the grace of God has been received. This is the focus of our study, and throughout our investigation we will see the need to act upon the grace we have been given. Although we did not receive the grace of God by our works, Revelation 2 and 3 tell us that Jesus knows our works. There is no contradiction in these verses, just a different emphasis of the gospel that the Holy Spirit wants us to see.

The reason we have not seen these distinctions before is the same reason we have not recognized the tares sown among the wheat—an enemy has done this (Matthew 13:28). We should not be surprised to see the sinister hand of Satan working behind the scenes to hide the gospel of the kingdom and the 1,000-year reign of Jesus Christ. Why he did this will be the focus of our next inquiry into "The Kingdom Lost."

CHAPTER 2
THE KINGDOM LOST

In this chapter we will examine how and why the truth of the 1,000-year reign of Jesus on the earth was lost. To do this, we will have to retrace the history of the church. As interesting as this may be, it may also be somewhat painful. I offer this advanced notice because we will find that Satan infiltrated the church and sowed his seeds of perverted doctrine to quench the Spirit of evangelism, and he tried to hide the coming age of Israel's re-emergence into world dominance. Why? Because this is the prophecy that comes to pass just before Satan's final fate in the lake of fire is fulfilled.

This took place comparatively early in church history and happened as a result of the Roman Catholic domination of the body of Christ. I offer this frank notation for the sake of the many wonderful Christians who function within the Roman Catholic Church whom I do not wish to hurt nor offend. Please do not feel singled out on account of this statement, but history does not lie. We will see that Jesus prophesied that this truth would be hidden. This loss of the knowledge of the millennial kingdom is well documented in history, especially in the *Roman Catholic Encyclopedia*. It is necessary to understand why this truth was lost in order to grasp its true significance and where it fits into end-time events.

The fact remains that the gospel of the kingdom is not taught in the Roman Catholic Church, nor in the vast majority of orthodox, protestant, evangelical, charismatic, or fundamental organizations. The church of Jesus Christ has a common enemy—Satan. We will see that he is the party responsible for this loss of truth, and that when we regain it, ours will be a common advance upon him who "sowed tares among the wheat."

The History of the Early Church

The early Christian church (during the first and second centuries after Christ) was evangelizing the world at a truly amazing rate. According to James H. Rutz in *The Open Church*, it is estimated that had this initial rate of evangelism gone unchecked, the entire world would have become evangelized by the year A.D. 600.[1] Not only was the church advancing over the world, but it was also becoming a threat to the established political power at the time—the Roman Empire. The reason Christianity was such a threat is because Christians were talking about their King, Jesus Christ, and His coming to establish a kingdom that would dominate the world, which is a major tenet of the gospel of the kingdom. The Scriptures document the stir this was causing.

> *And when they [sons of Belial] found them [Paul and Silas] not, they drew Jason and certain brethren unto the rulers of the city, crying, These that have turned the world upside down are come hither also; whom Jason hath received: and these all do contrary to the decrees of Caesar, saying that there is another king, one Jesus. And they troubled the people and the rulers of the city, when they heard these things.*   Acts 17:6–8

Roman officials were compelled to take some action to squelch these uprisings. Not only were Christians talking

The Kingdom Lost

about Jesus being King and looking for His coming, but they were also talking about another kingdom He would establish.

> *And in the days of these kings shall the God of heaven set up a kingdom, which shall never be destroyed: and the kingdom shall not be left to other people, but it shall break in pieces and consume all these kingdoms, and it shall stand for ever.* *Daniel 2:44*

Roman emperors began persecuting Christians, having them executed and even using their death as entertainment in the Roman Coliseum. Apparently this happened even during the Apostle Paul's lifetime. First Corinthians 15:32 recounts that Paul wrestled with beasts at Ephesus. Whether these were actual beasts or figurative ones, Paul used the promise of his future inheritance as inner strength to face this trial.

> *If after the manner of men I have fought with beasts at Ephesus, what advantageth it me, if the dead rise not? Let us eat and drink; for to morrow we die.* *1 Corinthians 15:32*

During the time period of the first through third centuries, political instability threatened to undermine the Roman Empire. In an attempt to counteract the unrest, the Caesars persecuted Christians. The blood of the martyrs watered the seeds of the gospel of the kingdom, however, causing a result opposite to that intended. These martyrs were also promoted into a guaranteed inheritance of the 1,000-year reign, which is another salient truth concerning the gospel of the kingdom.

> *And I saw thrones, and they sat upon them, and judgment was given unto them: and I saw the souls of them that were beheaded for the witness of Jesus, and for the word of God, and which had not worshipped the beast, neither his image, neither had received*

> *his mark upon their foreheads, or in their hands; and they lived and reigned with Christ a thousand years.   Revelation 20:4*

Note: A reward in the coming kingdom for martyrdom is a fundamental doctrine of Christianity. Mohammed, the prophet of Islam, adopted this into the Islamic faith, but he stole the idea from the Bible and has millions of Muslims motivated by it. His perversion of martyrdom has Muslims supposedly going straight into paradise if they die in their Jihad (holy war). If the church would teach the genuine truth of the gospel of the kingdom, the church would have more incentive for living and dying for the faith too. Giving one's life for the furtherance of the kingdom is exactly what Jesus taught his disciples—whoever loses his life for the kingdom's sake will gain it.[2]

The Roman emperor Diocletian (A.D. 284–305) killed more Christians than all the others before him, but this only seemed to intensify the problem of this growing sect of Christians. The succeeding emperor, Constantine (A.D. 288–337), could see that persecuting Christians was not working, so in a diabolical move calculated to halt the spread of true Christianity, he undermined the gospel of the kingdom. Constantine decided that if he could not kill them off, then he would buy them off.[3] Constantine contrived an idea which would unite the empire and at the same time quell the uprising of Christians.

Constantine, hailed by many as a founding father of Christianity, was not primarily a strong believer,[4] but he was an astute politician who used religion to unite the Roman Empire. He had his leaders develop a universal (catholic) religion to include the beliefs of all citizens of Rome, including those of Egypt, Greece, Asia Minor, and the Bible lands. By a process called syncretism, he began merging different pagan beliefs alongside Christianity into a common Roman universal religion, ultimately known as the Roman

Catholic Church. When Constantine initiated the Roman universal church with one lethal stroke of his pen, he effectively removed the incentive for evangelism and killed the growth of Christianity. By his decree from the Council of Nicea in A.D. 325, Christians no longer needed to witness, because the entire Roman Empire was now Christian, or to be more accurate, they had become catholic—members of the new universal religion.

Instead of persecuting Christians now, Constantine encouraged them to become catholic. He built large cathedrals for the benefit of all the new members and lavished them with ornate services and, of course, appointed his hand-picked leaders to high-ranking positions within the priesthood. He did have to kill off a number of dissenters, but for the most part, the new Roman Catholic (universal) Church watered down Christianity to the point that one could be born again within it, but the truth of the gospel of the kingdom was quietly neglected long enough to fade into a forgotten concept. Our enemy, the devil, worked through Constantine and others, as we will see, to deliver this crippling blow to true Christianity.

The purpose of this exposé is not to criticize Constantine or the Roman Catholic Church, but to determine how we lost the understanding and teachings of the 1,000-year reign of Jesus on the earth. Many sincere Christians are in the Roman Catholic Church, but likewise, many pagans are in it as well. It is a universal belief system that anyone can embrace, but it is as political as it is religious, and it is a mingled version of many beliefs. By virtue of this brilliant political strategy from Constantine, Christians were no longer witnessing the truth of eternal life through Jesus Christ, but were enjoying the ornate trappings of the new cathedrals and seeking to please the church instead of God. Even though the impetus for witnessing had been removed, the truth about a coming kingdom still surfaced from time to time and needed to be put down. So, the next major move of Satan to kill the gospel of the kingdom was not political, but doctrinal. It came through Augustine, probably the most influential theologian since the Apostle Paul.

Naturally it was not in the best interests of the Roman Empire, and now its universal church (controlled and financed by the empire), to recognize any biblical prophecy that foretold a coming kingdom would crush the Roman Empire and would reign in its stead. So, the Roman church found a theologian who embraced a philosophy that would hide the kingdom of heaven.

In *Heaven, the Mystery of Angels*, Grant Jeffrey writes:

> As the Church became involved with emperors like Constantine (288–337), who supported Christianity, it began to take on political status. The belief in the actual return of Christ quickly faded away. Naturally, a Roman Emperor like Constantine did not look with favor on the biblical prophecy that all Gentile world empires would be overthrown by the Second Coming of Christ. Augustine (354–430), the most influential theologian since Paul, began to teach that the Return of Christ, the Battle of Armageddon, and the Millennium were allegories to be understood only symbolically. In his book, *The City of God*, he denied a future millennium with Christ's return and reign. Tragically, this denial of the Scriptures set the tone for the majority of Catholic and Protestant theologians for centuries to come.[5]

The continuum of church history shows us that at the time of the Reformation, Martin Luther and other leaders recovered only the gospel of grace and not the gospel of the kingdom. Protestants have regained the truth that people are saved through faith, by the grace of God, but the gospel of the kingdom is still, for the most part, lying dormant, as a sleeping giant ready to be roused.

This truth of the 1,000-year reign of Jesus on the earth gave the early church incentive to strive for the masteries and the coming kingdom. When this truth is regained, the same momentum it gave to the early church to risk their lives for the sake of their true King will come to us again.

We will see in chapter 6, "The Inheritances of Grace and Reward," that Jesus prophesied in Matthew 13 that the gospel of the kingdom would be lost during the church age. We have seen that it was accomplished politically to explain away the coming reign of a greater kingdom than the Roman Empire. We must realize that it was the hand of Satan behind this and *not* people. He was trying to obscure the incentive Christians needed to push ahead in the face of persecution; he was afraid of the gospel of the kingdom then, and he is afraid of it now.

There is a promise of the 1,000-year reign of Jesus coming to the earth, and those individuals who show themselves faithful will be allowed to live and reign with Him too. There is no question about the truth of this kingdom having been lost and therefore not being emphasized in Bible teachings and Christian educational curricula.

This doctrine needs to be explicitly understood. In order to do this and rebuild the truth that was lost, we need to study the time period of the 1,000-year reign of Jesus on the earth and see exactly when it occurs in the framework of God's plans. We will do this in the next chapter, "The Outline of the Ages."

CHAPTER 3
The Outline of the Ages

Perhaps one of the first lessons we should have been taught when we first tried to understand the Bible was an outline of the ages. In every exposé, the questions of who, what, where, when, why, and how need to be covered, and this subject from the Bible is no exception. Even though we are focusing on how we can enter into the millennial reign with Jesus, we have already seen why it was lost. Now we will examine when the millennial kingdom will occur and where it fits into the overall flow of God's timetable and end-time prophecy.

There are a number of ages revealed in Scripture, and to understand where the millennial kingdom fits into them, we must lay out the whole scope of God's plans and timing. Nowhere else in the whole Bible is this outline more clearly laid out than in 2 Peter 3. This section of the Word of God is an overview of history (His story) that shows three distinct ages. There is the former, the present, and the latter. We will see that the millennial reign of Jesus occurs at the end of the present age in which we are living and will usher in the next heavens and earth.

Second Peter 3 was written to rebuke any scoffer who denies the literal fulfillment of the coming events of end-time

The Outline of the Ages

prophecy. It not only discloses the millennial kingdom and where it fits into the end-time sequence but also the whole scope of the ages and the certainty of coming events.

> *Knowing this first, that there shall come in the last days scoffers, walking after their own lusts, and saying, Where is the promise of his coming? For since the fathers fell asleep, all things continue as they were from the beginning of the creation.*   *2 Peter 3:3–4*

Verses 5 and 6 show the former age and heavens and earth.

> *For this they willingly are ignorant of, that by the word of God the heavens were of old, and the earth standing out of the water and in the water: Whereby the world that then was, being overflowed with water, perished.*
>   *2 Peter 3:5–6*

This age or period of time refers to the history of the earth when it was standing in the midst of water, and God had to reconstruct the heavens and earth. This is referenced in Genesis 1:1–10 where God divided the dry land from the water in the firmament and on the face of the earth. Many Bible scholars believe that the original heavens and earth was destroyed when Lucifer (now Satan) attempted mutiny. They teach that his ousting destroyed the original creation and caused the entire cosmos to need revamping.[1]

Other Bible teachers believe that 2 Peter 3:5 and 6 refer to the time of Noah when the earth was destroyed by the flood. There are some valid points of reasoning behind this belief too, but the matter at hand deals with the fact that there are three distinct, separate ages covering the whole story of mankind and earth. We are more concerned with the one that is existing now and the one yet to come in the future.

The second, or present age, is the one in which we are living now. This is documented by 2 Peter 3:7.

> *But the heavens and the earth, which are now, by the same word are kept in store, reserved unto fire against the day of judgment and perdition of ungodly men.*
> *2 Peter 3:7*

There is no doubt that the one we are in now is the one that says *now*. The present heavens and earth will be preserved unto the day when God will destroy them with fire. After the heavens and earth that exist now are destroyed by fire, the new heavens and earth will be created. This is the age of the future.

> *Nevertheless we, according to his promise, look for new heavens and a new earth, wherein dwelleth righteousness.*
> *2 Peter 3:13*

The understanding of these ages is important, because it will allow us to ascertain a position on God's timeline for the millennial kingdom. We can deduce that it will occur at the end of the second (now) heavens and earth, and just before the creation of the third (future) one. In other words, the millennial kingdom will exist on earth just before the "now" heavens and earth are destroyed by fire.

> *And when the thousand years are expired, Satan shall be loosed out of his prison, and shall go out to deceive the nations which are in the four quarters of the earth, Gog, and Magog, to gather them together to battle: the number of whom is as the sand of the sea. And they went up on the breadth of the earth, and compassed the camp of the saints about, and the beloved city: and fire came down from God out of heaven, and devoured them.*
> *Revelation 20:7–9*

The fire that will come down out of heaven and devour them is the same fire that burns with brimstone and will purify the earth. This is the fire that has been held in store to judge the earth along with all the ungodly men and women on it. The important fact to retain from all of this is that the heavens and earth existing now will house the millennial kingdom and at the end of the thousand years, those who will be judged by fire. Then the new heavens and earth will be brought into existence. In other words, the fleeing away of the heavens and earth that are now (2 Peter 3:7–10) and the burning of it (2 Peter 3:10 and 12) precede the new heavens and earth (Revelation 21:1).

This insight is crucial because of an unsubstantiated belief in Christianity that when someone dies they go to heaven and, as far as the belief goes, that's it. This is not doctrinal and it's not true. There are many other details that the Bible clearly reveals, one of which is the millennial kingdom. Most people think that they start the "heaven trip" and go immediately to Revelation 21 and 22 as soon as they die. Again, this is not true. The new heavens and earth of Revelation 21 and 22 do not exist yet, and they will not exist until the present heavens and earth are destroyed with fire at the end of the millennial kingdom.

Another Christian may acclaim the "rapture of the church" as their final destiny. This also is not accurate according to Scripture, because even after the rapture takes place, the church must pass through the judgment seat of Christ. There individuals will either receive their prize for faithfulness—the millennial reign, or punishment for infidelity and/or laziness—the outer darkness. Those who do receive the prize for faithfulness will attend the marriage supper of the Lamb and descend to the earth with the Lord in His army where they will establish His kingdom for a thousand years. We will see that those who have not been faithful will have to sit out the next thousand years and wait for the new heavens and earth. It is only after the millennial kingdom that the new heavens and earth will come to exist.

Second Peter 3:8 reveals another piece of the puzzle which documents the timing of the millennial kingdom. Verse 8 asserts the existence of the heavens and earth that are now and offers an interesting clue to the duration of this heavens and earth.

> *But, beloved, be not ignorant of this one thing, that one day is with the Lord as a thousand years, and a thousand years as one day.*
> *2 Peter 3:8*

This scripture tells us that a thousand years is as one day with the Lord. Since there are seven days in a week, this gives rise to discussion of the week of millennia—a week consisting of seven days, with each day being a thousand years long.

The Week of Millennia

Even though we are discussing an outline of the ages, the week of millennia is pertinent to our investigation because it is the full story of the heavens and earth that are now. The week of millennia specifies that the Lord has put a 7,000-year lease on this piece of real estate we call earth. This 7,000-year period is composed of seven days of a thousand years each or the week of millennia.

This week of millennia is more than just a theory. It is well documented in the Bible and is reflected in ancient writings that predate the hiding of the gospel of the kingdom. First, God said to Adam that in the day you eat (from the tree of the knowledge of good and evil), you will surely die. Adam died at the age of 930, still within that (first) day of the week of millennia when he ate of the fruit. It is no coincidence that the last day of this week, when the millennial reign occurs, is 1,000 years in length, too. The reason being that it is the last day of the week allotted for the present heavens and earth.

The Outline of the Ages

All biblical reckoning of time dates our existence right now around the 6,000-year mark from the time of Adam in the heavens and earth that currently exist. The breakdown of this week and the days of the week is amazing.

- Adam was born on the first day of the week, circa 4000 B.C.

- Noah was born at the beginning of the second day, circa 3000 B.C.

- Abraham was born at the beginning of the third day, circa 2000 B.C.

- David was born near the beginning of the fourth day, circa 1000 B.C.

- Jesus was born at the beginning of the fifth day, circa A.D. 1.

The first four days make up the first part of the week, and the next two days of this week comprise what is called the latter or last days. The latter days are from A.D. 1 to circa A.D. 2000.

> *And it shall come to pass in the last days, saith God, I will pour out of my Spirit upon all flesh: and your sons and your daughters shall prophesy, and your young men shall see visions, and your old men shall dream dreams.*
> *Acts 2:17*

> *Hath in these last days spoken unto us by his Son, whom he hath appointed heir of all things, by whom also he made the worlds.*
> *Hebrews 1:2*

Notice that it says "last days" (plural) making this two-day period of time a unit. These are the days of the Gentile priesthood or the mystery era, which will precede the very last day, or the Sabbath of the week of millennia—the 1,000-year reign of Jesus on the earth. Hebrews 4:9 refers to this day.

> *There remaineth therefore a rest [sabbatismos] to the people of God.*   *Hebrews 4:9*

This word, *sabbatismos* (sabbath), refers to the coming rest for God's people and is known as the millennial kingdom. It is the fulfillment of God's promise to His people concerning the coming glory of Jesus on the earth. It is also known as the Lord's Day. The apostle John said,

> *I was in the Spirit on the Lord's day, and heard behind me a great voice, as of a trumpet.*
> *Revelation 1:10*

This does not mean that John was in the Spirit on Saturday, Sunday, or any other particular day of the week.[2] It means that he went into the spirit realm and was shown the things that would usher the day of the Lord (the final culminating day of the week of millennia) into existence on the earth.

So, in synopsis of our understanding of the ages and the week of millennia, there are three ages dealing with the heavens and the earth—the first (past), second (now), and third (future). We are living in the second age now, and it consists of seven days of 1,000 years each. So far we have passed through 6,000 years or six days; so sometime very, very soon the day of the Lord will commence. We are about to see the establishing of this kingdom; therefore, the importance of understanding this kingdom and the criterion for entering it is that much more intensified. The new heavens and earth, or our eternal, permanent home, will be created at the end of the 1,000-year reign of Jesus on the earth.

There is so much confusion about end-time events within the church today. Quite honestly, most Christians, according to what they are taught or not taught, do not even recognize that we are living in the end time of this sixth day of the week. They scarcely know about the imminent rapture of the church, much less the millennial kingdom that will exist afterward on this earth.

This confusion can be straightened out as we continue our study of the 1,000-reign of the Lord on the earth. Out of necessity we will cover the order of end-time events, going through the gathering together of the church, the judgment seat of Christ, and into the millennial reign of Jesus on this earth. We need to understand that this reign of Jesus will be here upon the earth, so all the talk about the earth being exploded by nuclear threat or the environment wasting away amounts to idle words when compared to the prophecy of the Bible.

Still, our greater focus is not merely to intellectually understand these matters, but to live according to the standard that the Lord requires for us to enter into this kingdom. Our further quest in this section, "The Kingdom Explained," is to explore the truth that this kingdom will be upon the earth and will be given to those who merit it by faithfulness and service. We are somewhat familiar with the sufferings Jesus endured when He was crucified, but as Paul Harvey says, now we can learn "the rest of the story" as we glimpse the glory of the Lord that will be revealed. We are about to see the promise of the day of the Lord unfold soon, and the Lord will begin His reign upon the earth.

CHAPTER 4
Understanding the End-Time Sequence of Events

Too many Christians are confused by the rapture of the church versus the Lord's return to the earth to establish the kingdom promised by God. We could easily differentiate between them and give them each a definition, but a far greater truth is lying beneath the surface. This is not easy to grasp because the explanation includes the greatest mystery the world has ever known. It is the *great mystery* which God hid within Himself. It behooves us to discover this great secret and why God originally hid it from the whole world.

There is no doubt that Jesus is coming to earth to establish His kingdom. It always has been, and is still being prophesied (Daniel 2:44). Jesus will come to the earth, set foot on the Mount of Olives (Zechariah 14:1–4), and begin His rulership over all the world. The Jews knew of it and/or still know it, but when the King came the first time to do this, they rejected Him, killed Him, and did not allow Him to set up His kingdom. As much as their rejection of Him complicated the plan, an additional problem arose since the Jews were supposed to reign with Him, too.

God, in His omniscience, knew this would happen and had an alternate plan waiting in the wings. This plan is called the "great mystery." Because this great mystery (which includes the gathering together or rapture of the church) was never revealed until sometime in the first century to the Apostle Paul, there is much confusion concerning the sequencing of end-time events. No one knew about this period of time until God threw the devil His curve ball.

> *But we speak the wisdom of God in a [regarding the] mystery, even the hidden wisdom, which God ordained before the world unto our glory: which none of the princes of this world knew: for had they known it, they would not have crucified the Lord of glory.*
> *1 Corinthians 2:7–8*

So while studying this may be a little inconvenient, it will be beneficial because God foreordained this great mystery to our glory. Peter even said these things are hard to understand.

> *And account that the longsuffering of our Lord is salvation; even as our beloved brother Paul also according to the wisdom given unto him hath written unto you; as also in all his epistles, speaking in them of these things; in which are some things hard to be understood, which they that are unlearned and unstable wrest, as they do also the other scriptures, unto their own destruction.   2 Peter 3:15–16*

But notice quickly the concluding verses of 2 Peter that unveil to us the benefits of knowing this and studying it.

> *Ye therefore, beloved, seeing ye know these things before, beware lest ye also, being led away with the error of the wicked, fall from your own stedfastness.   2 Peter 3:17*

The final verse of this chapter gives us direct guidance and also one last piece of information about the millennial kingdom. The last phrase should be translated, "To Him be glory both now and in the age to come."

> *But grow in grace, and in the knowledge of our Lord and Saviour Jesus Christ. To him be glory both now and for ever [the age to come]. Amen.*   *2 Peter 3:18*

So let's begin our study to clarify the sequence of end-time events and to differentiate between the rapture of the church off the earth and the coming of the Lord to the earth to establish the kingdom. A summary of the sequence of end-time events is as follows:

1. At God's appointed time, the church will be evacuated off the planet.

2. The church will go up to meet the Lord in the air and will pass through the judgment seat of Christ while the world endures the great tribulation and finally the wrath of God.

3. Those who pass through the judgment seat of Christ, along with those who are saved during the great tribulation and those of the resurrection of the just, will be chosen as the bride of Christ and will return to the earth with the Lord to establish His kingdom.

In explaining the great mystery and the sequence of end-time events, we shall also see the need for the church to be evacuated off the earth so that the remaining prophecies concerning Israel and the soon coming kingdom can be fulfilled.

The Gathering of the Church

The gathering together of the church or, as many people call it, the rapture, is only the beginning of the end-times sequence. This marks the termination of a Gentile priesthood and the re-emergence of Israel's role in receiving their Messiah and ultimately reigning with the Lord Jesus Christ. The gathering together of the church is not prophesied anywhere in the Old Testament because it is part of the great mystery that was hidden.

> *For the Lord himself shall descend from heaven with a shout, with the voice of the archangel, and with the trump of God: and the dead in Christ shall rise first: Then we which are alive and remain shall be caught up together with them in the clouds, to meet the Lord in the air: and so shall we ever be with the Lord.*   *1 Thessalonians 4:16–17*

Notice that the Lord does not set foot upon the earth, but the church goes up in the air to meet Him. The church goes to heaven and is taken out of the way (2 Thessalonians 2:7) so that the prophecies given to the nation of Israel can be fulfilled. When the church is taken off the earth, that event terminates the Gentile priesthood and ends the great mystery period.

> *For I would not, brethren, that ye should be ignorant of this mystery, lest ye should be wise in your own conceits; that blindness in part is happened to Israel, until the fullness of the Gentiles be come in.*   *Romans 11:25*

When the church leaves, which is synonymous with the fullness of the Gentiles coming in, the 70th week of Daniel (Daniel 9:24) or the great tribulation (Revelation 7:14), also known as Jacob's trouble (Jeremiah 30:7), can take place. The blindness of heart that will have happened to Israel will end, and they will begin to see who their Messiah is. The rapture is foretold in Revelation 4:1.

The 1,000 Year Reign of Jesus Christ on the Earth

> *After this I looked, and, behold, a door was opened in heaven: and the first voice which I heard was as it were of a trumpet talking with me; which said, Come up hither, and I will shew thee things which must be hereafter. And immediately I was in the spirit: and, behold, a throne was set in heaven, and one sat on the throne.*   *Revelation 4:1–2*

The church "goes up hither" with the trumpet (1 Thessalonians 4:16–17) by the call of the voice of the archangel. They go in the spirit to the throne of God in the heavens. Then the remaining events of the 70th week of Daniel, the seven years of great tribulation, will transpire.

Of course there are many details in the book of Revelation, but its highlights point to the coming of the Lord to the earth. The 144,000 Jewish evangelists (Revelation 7:4) testify along with the two witnesses (Revelation 11:2ff) and win multitudes before the harvest at the end of the world (Revelation 14). These individuals will be in the millennial kingdom because they will be raised at the resurrection of the just (Revelation 20:4–5).

The ensuing events, basically from Revelation 15–18, give an account of the wrath of God poured out upon those who choose to reject God and receive the mark of the beast. The return of the Lord to the earth in Revelation 19 provides specific information about the coming millennial kingdom.

The bride of Christ is chosen out of the body of Christ and is given a white wedding garment (Revelation 19:7–8). The marriage supper of the Lamb is prepared and celebrated just before the Lord leaves with His bride to return to the earth to save Israel from the antichrist (Revelation 19:17–21). Those who return with Jesus on white horses are the ones chosen to reign with Him on the earth. Once the antichrist and his army are defeated and the devil is bound for a thousand years,

Understanding the End-Time Sequence of Events

those who returned out of heaven with the Lord will begin establishing His kingdom on the earth for the next 1,000 years.

The point to note here is that the gathering together of the church happens *before* the Lord's return to the earth. The church that passes through the judgment seat of Christ (those who receive their reward for faithfulness), along with righteous Israel from the Old Testament, and those saved out of the great tribulation will compose the army of the Lord. These will be the ones returning with the Lord to establish His kingdom on the earth.

In other writings, an immense amount of detailed attention has been given to the events during the seven-year period of tribulation. However, the focus of this book is the 1,000 years to follow. This 1,000-year period is the prophesied reign of Jesus Christ from Jerusalem. This 1,000-year period is the fulfillment of the promise of the Lord's glory.

We must not forget that, at the end of the 1,000-year reign of Jesus on the earth, the devil will be loosed for a short season (Revelation 20:7–9). After his attempt at rebellion is again thwarted, he will be banished forever into the lake of fire. At this point the earth will be cleansed by fire, and the third (or new) heavens and earth will be created. Hallelujah!

The end of the millennial kingdom will mark the end of the second heavens and earth and the beginning of the next heavens and earth. This is important because we will see that those born-again individuals who did not prove themselves worthy to reign during the 1,000 years will still have an inheritance of grace in the new heavens and earth. We will better understand the great significance of the next age when we study the subject of our "inheritances."

Before moving into our examination of inheritances, we need to consider the sufferings and glory of the Lord. This truth parallels the time sequence and revelation of the great mystery, and is necessary to fully appreciate the Father's will—that Jesus and all His followers receive the glory rightfully due them. We will study this in the next chapter, "The Sufferings and the Glory of the Lord."

CHAPTER 5
THE SUFFERINGS AND THE GLORY OF THE LORD

Now that we have laid a foundation for the outline of the ages and the sequence of end-time events, we can embrace the true passion of our subject. The Lord Jesus Christ is the King of glory and has never been recognized by His own people, Israel; thus, the people of the world have not honored Him. God the Father will defend His honor—Jesus suffered; He must be glorified.

The gathering together of the church does not represent the fullness of the Lord's glory. The church will rise to meet the Lord in the air and be in heaven with Him, but only for a short duration. After taking the church through the judgment seat of Christ and choosing His bride, the Lord will return to the earth. His glory will not be fully realized in the heavens as the Lamb Who has prevailed to unroll the scrolls. He deserves honor from all the peoples of the earth as the true King of glory.

> *And the glory of the LORD shall be revealed, and all flesh shall see it together: for the mouth of the LORD hath spoken it.*   Isaiah 40:5

The sufferings of the Lord took place on this earth, and His glory will also take place on this same terra firma. He is coming in glory and righteousness to rule and establish God's kingdom in justice and power. He has been promised to sit on His Father's throne and rule over the earth. He was nailed to the cross on Golgotha, but He will come again and touch down on a higher plane—the Mount of Olives!

> *And his feet shall stand in that day upon the mount of Olives, which is before Jerusalem on the east, and the mount of Olives shall cleave in the midst thereof toward the east and toward the west, and there shall be a very great valley; and half of the mountain shall remove toward the north, and half of it toward the south.*   Zechariah 14:4

Yes, the Lord is coming again to the earth to establish the kingdom of His Father and to reign on the earth for 1,000 years. Amillenarians may treat the return of the Lord Jesus Christ to the earth as an allegory, but it was Jesus, not an allegory, that came the first time. Jesus will sit on the throne of His Father in Jerusalem. This was prophesied in Daniel and Isaiah.

> *And in the days of these kings shall the God of heaven set up a kingdom, which shall never be destroyed: and the kingdom shall not be left to other people, but it shall break in pieces and consume all these kingdoms, and it shall stand for ever.*   Daniel 2:44

> *For unto us a child is born, unto us a son is given: and the government shall be upon his shoulder: and his name shall be called Wonderful, Counsellor, The mighty God, The everlasting Father, The Prince of Peace. Of the increase of his government and peace there shall be no end, upon the throne of David, and*

> *upon his kingdom, to order it, and to establish it with judgment and with justice from henceforth even for ever. The zeal of the LORD of hosts will perform this. Isaiah 9:6–7*

Furthermore, it is prophesied in the book of Revelation that this kingdom shall come to the earth.

> *And hast made us unto our God kings and priests: and we shall reign on the earth.*
> *Revelation 5:10*

Jesus' return to the earth is not an allegory—He suffered here; He will be glorified here.

Understanding the Sufferings and the Glory of the Lord

Every sincere Bible believer knows that Jesus' story line is still missing a major section—the crescendo and conclusion. Even now we are waiting to see Him crowned and glorified as King. The Old Testament prophets searched for the time that deals with Christ's glory. The Spirit has amply testified of the sufferings of the Lord, but it also testifies of the glory that shall be revealed.

We have read in our Bibles about the mental torment, the beatings, ridicule, and crucifixion that our Lord endured. We have seen how He opened not His mouth, but was as a sheep going to the slaughter. We have wept; we shall yet rejoice. The Bible testifies that Jesus has a glory yet to be revealed— He is coming again, not as a suffering shepherd, but as a glorified King! This is the glory of His reign on the earth as the King from heaven.

Sufferings and glory are dual realities that parallel the comings of the Lord. He came to suffer on the earth the first time, and He is coming again to the earth to reign in all the resplendent glory of His Father. The sufferings and the glory have both been prophesied.

It is interesting to note that the sufferings and glory foretold in Genesis, Isaiah, Jeremiah, and Ezekiel, etc., were also foretold in the Word of God written in the heavenlies long before the written Scriptures came to be. There are three main chapter divisions in the story line written in the heavenlies.[1]

- The first is the suffering of the Messiah.
- The second is the price paid for redemption.
- The third is the Messiah coming in glory.

This is the message that is uttered (Psalm 19:1–4) "day after day and night unto night." God wants all men and women to know that even though Jesus suffered, some day He *will* be glorified. He plastered these messages in the heavenlies for all to see. This is not an allegory. Someday the Lord will return and establish a glorious kingdom that will surpass all others. Our privilege and challenge remains—to prove ourselves qualified to enter into this kingdom. I don't want to miss it!

In the previous chapter we covered the subject of the great mystery. It is necessary to briefly cover again some of the truths about it because this relates to the time period we are living in now—the bridge between the sufferings and glory. God kept the great mystery secret from before the foundations of the world (Romans 16:25; 1 Corinthians 2:7–8; Ephesians 3:5) and held it in reserve because He wanted to allow Israel the opportunity to accept Jesus as their King. Old Testament prophets searched for this period, yet could not find it.

> *Of which salvation the prophets have enquired and searched diligently, who prophesied of the grace that should come unto you: Searching what, or what manner of time the Spirit of*

The Sufferings and the Glory of the Lord

> *Christ which was in them did signify, when it testified beforehand the sufferings of Christ, and the glory that should follow.*
> *1 Peter 1:10–11*

They could see a period of grace coming at some point in time, but they did not know the fullness of what it would involve. This era of grace, from God's point of view, was to be the time when He would give everyone on the earth an opportunity to embrace His plan of redemption—not just Israel. This period is called the mystery era or the age of the Gentile priesthood. Romans 11:25 mentions this period of time and the Gentile priesthood.

> *For I would not, brethren, that ye should be ignorant of this mystery, lest ye should be wise in your own conceits; that blindness in part is happened to Israel, until the fullness of the Gentiles be come in.*   *Romans 11:25*

The fullness of the Gentiles will be achieved when all the Gentiles who are called by God's election have come to a saving knowledge of Jesus Christ. Israel, for the most part, has been blind to the plan of redemption concerning Jesus of Nazareth as the true Messiah whom God ordained and sent. When all the Gentiles have been saved and gathered together unto the Lord, the priesthood of the Gentiles and the mystery era will end. This milestone will be marked by the gathering together, or rapture, of the church when believers in Christ will be raised from the dead and those who are alive and remain will be caught up in the air to meet the Lord.

From the birthing of the church on the day of Pentecost until the gathering together of the church, the Holy Spirit has been calling out individual Gentiles and giving each an opportunity to (1) get saved, and then (2) demonstrate worthiness to enter into the final glory reign of the Messiah on the earth.

The 1,000 Year Reign of Jesus Christ on the Earth

When the disciples asked the Lord in Acts 1:6 if He was going to restore the kingdom to Israel, that was a perfectly good question. They did not know about the intervening period between the sufferings of Jesus and the glory that would follow.

> *So when they met together, they asked him, "Lord, are you at this time going to restore the kingdom to Israel?"* Acts 1:6

They wanted to know if Jesus was going to get on a white horse, ride through the streets of Jerusalem, and break the oppression of the Roman Empire off them. Jesus, in His customarily brilliant response, prophesied of the era in which we have been living for the past 2,000 years.

> *He said to them: "It is not for you to know the times or dates the Father has set by his own authority. But you will receive power when the Holy Spirit comes on you; and you will be my witnesses in Jerusalem, and in all Judea and Samaria, and to the ends of the earth."* Acts 1:7–8 NKJ

During this period of time we are living in now, the Holy Spirit has been calling out the Gentiles elected by God. But when the church is taken off the earth, or as 2 Thessalonians 2:7 says, "when He [the Holy Spirit] is taken out of the way," the nation of Israel will again re-emerge as a nation to lead the world to repentance and into accepting Jesus as Messiah and the coming King of glory.

The past 2,000 years have been an extended grace period to allow anyone to become a priest before the Lord and to give them all an opportunity to demonstrate their response and faithfulness to the call of God. This period is Thursday and Friday of the week of millennia, and the weekend is about to start. The weekend is called the day of the Lord and also the glory of the Lord.

The Sufferings and the Glory of the Lord

Peter knew about the day when the Lord Jesus would be glorified in the future.

> *The elders which are among you I exhort, who am also an elder, and a witness of the sufferings of Christ, and also a partaker of the glory that shall be revealed.*   1 Peter 5:1

Peter watched them beat Jesus in the courtyard of the High Priest. He watched them ridicule and slap Him. The bloodied face of Jesus looked at Peter when he denied Him the third time. Peter knew that someday this same Jesus would return and establish His kingdom on the earth. His glory would then be revealed.

Psalm 2 tells of the day of the Lord and His glory. In the beginning of the chapter we see the heathen imagining a vain thing, trying to stop the counsel of the Lord from coming to pass.

> *Yet have I set my king upon my holy hill of Zion. I will declare the decree: the LORD hath said unto me, Thou art my Son; this day have I begotten thee. Ask of me, and I shall give thee the heathen for thine inheritance, and the uttermost parts of the earth for thy possession. Thou shalt break them with a rod of iron; thou shalt dash them in pieces like a potter's vessel. Be wise now therefore, O ye kings: be instructed, ye judges of the earth. Serve the LORD with fear, and rejoice with trembling. Kiss the Son, lest he be angry, and ye perish from the way, when his wrath is kindled but a little. Blessed are all they that put their trust in him.*   Psalm 2:6–12

Likewise, Psalm 24 tells of the King of glory and His reign on the earth.

> *Lift up your heads, O ye gates; and be ye lift up, ye everlasting doors; and the King of glory shall come in. Who is this King of glory? The LORD strong and mighty, the LORD mighty in battle. Lift up your heads, O ye gates; even lift them up, ye everlasting doors; and the King of glory shall come in. Who is this King of glory? The LORD of hosts, he is the King of glory. Selah.*   *Psalm 24:7–10*

The whole chapter of Psalm 47 declares the glorious reign of Jesus on the earth.

> *For the LORD most high is terrible; he is a great King over all the earth. He shall subdue the people under us, and the nations under our feet.*   *Psalm 47:2–3*

Isaiah 11 tells of His glorious reign, too.

> *And there shall come forth a rod out of the stem of Jesse, and a Branch shall grow out of his roots: And the spirit of the LORD shall rest upon him, the spirit of wisdom and understanding, the spirit of counsel and might, the spirit of knowledge and of the fear of the LORD; And shall make him of quick understanding in the fear of the LORD: and he shall not judge after the sight of his eyes, neither reprove after the hearing of his ears: But with righteousness shall he judge the poor, and reprove with equity for the meek of the earth: and he shall smite the earth: with the rod of his mouth, and with the breath of his lips shall he slay the wicked. And righteousness shall be the girdle of his loins, and faithfulness the girdle of his reins.*   *Isaiah 11:1–5*

The world has witnessed Jesus' sufferings and will yet behold His glory; the Word of God tells us that if we are willing to suffer with Him, then we too will be glorified with Him.

> *For I reckon that the sufferings of this present time are not worthy to be compared with the glory which shall be revealed in us.*
> *Romans 8:18*

> *If we suffer, we shall also reign with him: if we deny him, he also will deny us.*
> *2 Timothy 2:12*

> *But rejoice, inasmuch as ye are partakers of Christ's sufferings; that, when his glory shall be revealed, ye may be glad also with exceeding joy.*
> *1 Peter 4:13*

Yes, there is a day coming—it is the day of the Lord. In that day, we shall see the glory of the Lord. We have beheld His sufferings; we shall behold His glory. We who suffer with Him will reign with Him, too.

Jesus Christ will return and establish His Father's kingdom. He will sit on His throne in Jerusalem and rule the world. We will study war no more (Micah 4:3). David will reign over Israel (Ezekiel 34:23–24). Jesus' 12 apostles will reign over the 12 tribes of Israel (Matthew 19:28), and His bride that returns to earth with Him will reign over the nations and cities He assigns to them (Luke 19:17–19).

The glory of the Lord and His 1,000-year reign is not an allegory or a figure of speech. In the last days, scoffers will come and say He is not coming. Unbelief did not stop Him from coming the first time—His kingdom will come to this earth. I know that my Redeemer lives and shall stand some day upon the earth. From one of the earliest books of the Bible ever penned, the book of Job, to the book of Revelation, where it says, "Come quickly Lord Jesus," a cry echoes in the heart of every believer who feels the injustice of the world. We lift up our heads and anticipate the manifestation of the sons of God (Romans 8:19). Our redemption draws nigh.

> *For I know that my redeemer liveth, and that*
> *he shall stand at the latter day upon the earth.*
> *Job 19:25*

SECTION TWO
UNDERSTANDING OUR INHERITANCES

While studying the topics in this section, it will serve us well to remember that 2 Peter 3:16 warns us that some of these things are hard to understand. Just as we have seen that there is a gospel of grace and a gospel of the kingdom, we should not be surprised to discover that there is more than one inheritance available for the child of God. Why not? Our God is rich and "gives us richly all things to enjoy," because not only is He no respecter of persons, but He has also promised to bless those who diligently seek Him.

Since we have only known of an inheritance given by grace, we have wrongly assumed that there is no other. This assumption has caused great confusion, as well as doctrinal disagreements, due to thinking that this single perspective of grace must be right and all others must be wrong. Nevertheless, God is multifaceted and though His Word is simple, it is also very deep.

In this section, chapter 6, "The Inheritances of Grace and Reward," describes the different inheritances available and the criterion for receiving each of them. Chapter 7, "The Bride Comes Out of the Body," resolves the apparent disparity between the bride and body of Christ. Chapter 8, "Reigning with the Lord," reveals exciting truths concerning the privilege of reigning with Jesus during His coming kingdom on earth. These three chapters will explain the different inheritances and lay a basis for our understanding of how to enter the 1,000-year reign with Jesus on the earth.

CHAPTER 6
THE INHERITANCES OF GRACE AND REWARD

Inheritances excite people, and rightfully so, because they are news of something good coming in the future. As with "The Two Gospels," the first chapter in section 1, there are two inheritances for the child of God. One is by grace; the other is a reward for service.

This subject of inheritances confused me for many years. I knew that by the grace of God I would receive an inheritance from God, not by my works nor by my merit. First Peter 1:3 and 4 document this.

> *Blessed be the God and Father of our Lord Jesus Christ, which according to his abundant mercy hath begotten us again unto a lively hope by the resurrection of Jesus Christ from the dead, to an inheritance incorruptible, and undefiled, and that fadeth not away, reserved in heaven for you.*   1 Peter 1:3–4

As simple and straightforward as these verses are, others on the same subject seem to cloud, confuse, and even contradict the matter.

> *And whatsoever ye do, do it heartily, as to the Lord, and not unto men; knowing that of the Lord ye shall receive the reward of the inheritance: for ye serve the Lord Christ.*
> *Colossians 3:23–24*

The solution here is the same as the explanation of the two gospels—there are two separate kingdoms and an inheritance for each one. By now we have a grasp on this subject and have realized that knowledge of only one of these kingdoms does not make you wrong in your understanding, but it makes you only partly right. We must look at both, and the criteria necessary for each, if we are going to view the whole picture and receive the fullness of what God has in store for us.

God the Father has a kingdom over which He will rule (Revelation 21–22). In this kingdom, His grace will be equally divided to all of His children (Revelation 21:7). He has been, is now, and will at that time be, no respecter of persons. Jesus the Messiah also has a kingdom where He will sit on the throne of His Father and will rule over the earth with a rod of iron (Revelation 19:15). He will reward those who are about the Father's business. The inheritance of the Father's kingdom comes by grace and the inheritance of the Son's kingdom comes by merited reward.

We will discuss the details of both inheritances as well as their dissimilarities to assure that they are, in fact, different facets of the promises of God. To display this more clearly, we will use a table with scripture references documenting each point.

The Inheritance of Grace in the Kingdom of the Father

The inheritance of grace is the promise of living in the new heavens and earth. This is eternal life, meaning life in the age that never ends. (See appendix F, "The Word 'Eternal.'")

The Inheritances of Grace and Reward

John 3:16 promises this, and to receive this blessing the person must believe.

> *For God so loved the world, that he gave his only begotten Son, that whosoever believeth in him should not perish, but have everlasting life.*   John 3:16

Titus 3:4–7 reveals that this is the inheritance from the Father, that it comes by grace and not of works, that it came by believing on Jesus, and that it is the true promise of eternal life.

> *But after that the kindness and love of God the Father] our Saviour toward man appeared, Not by works of righteousness which we have done, but according to his mercy he saved us, by the washing of regeneration, and renewing of the Holy Ghost; Which he [God the Father] shed on us abundantly through Jesus Christ our Saviour; That being justified by his [God the Father's] grace, we should be made heirs according to the hope of eternal life [in His kingdom].*   Titus 3:4–7

First Peter 1:3 and 4 reveal this inheritance is given by God the Father, is reserved in heaven, and can never be lost.

> *Blessed be the God and Father of our Lord Jesus Christ, which according to his abundant mercy hath begotten us again unto a lively hope by the resurrection of Jesus Christ from the dead, To an inheritance incorruptible, and undefiled, and that fadeth not away, reserved in heaven for you.*   1 Peter 1:3–4

This is the inheritance that comes by salvation of grace and is the gift of God—it is not earned.

> *For by grace are ye saved through faith; and that not of yourselves: it is the gift of God.*
> *Ephesians 2:8*

These truths are very well known since they belong to the gospel of grace and have been heralded around the world since the early church. However, when we see the inheritance of reward, it will become quite apparent that there are two gospels and two distinct inheritances as well.

The Inheritance of Reward in the Kingdom of the Son

The inheritance of reward is acquired by faithful service, not just by grace.

> *And whatsoever ye do, do it heartily, as to the Lord, and not unto men; Knowing that of the Lord ye shall receive the reward of the inheritance: for ye serve the Lord Christ. But he that doeth wrong shall receive for the wrong which he hath done: and there is no respect of persons.*
> *Colossians 3:23–25*

Notice that these verses reference working and doing—not receiving by grace. The inheritance of the kingdom of heaven is not received by believing, but by repenting.

> *From that time Jesus began to preach, and to say, Repent: for the kingdom of heaven is at hand.*
> *Matthew 4:17*

The promises of inheritances in Revelation 2 and 3 are often highly touted as blessings of grace. The clarion truth of all these promises is that they are given to those who overcome by working and standing faithful to the end. These promises are not given by grace, but are given to those who faithfully serve to build the kingdom while living on earth. That is why

The Inheritances of Grace and Reward

each of these begins with the statement, "I know your works." Notice that there is a requirement: to hear what the Holy Spirit is saying to the churches. These promises are given to those who hear, obey, and then faithfully press into the kingdom of heaven.

> *He that hath an ear, let him hear what the Spirit saith unto the churches; To him that overcometh will I give to eat of the tree of life, which is in the midst of the paradise of God.*
> *Revelation 2:7*

> *He that hath an ear, let him hear what the Spirit saith unto the churches; He that overcometh shall not be hurt of the second death.*   *Revelation 2:11*

> *He that hath an ear, let him hear what the Spirit saith unto the churches; To him that overcometh will I give to eat of the hidden manna, and will give him a white stone, and in the stone a new name written, which no man knoweth saving he that receiveth it.*
> *Revelation 2:17*

> *He that overcometh, the same shall be clothed in white raiment; and I will not blot out his name out of the book of life [for the kingdom of the Son], but I will confess his name before my Father, and before his angels.   Revelation 3:5*

> *Him that overcometh will I make a pillar in the temple of my God, and he shall go no more out: and I will write upon him the name of my God, and the name of the city of my God, which is new Jerusalem, which cometh down out of heaven from my God: and I will write upon him my new name.*   *Revelation 3:12*

> *To him that overcometh will I grant to sit with me in my throne, even as I also overcame, and am set down with my Father in his throne.*
> *Revelation 3:21*

These are promises given to people who faithfully serve, as Colossians 3:24 says, "Ye shall receive the reward of the inheritance: for ye serve the Lord Christ."

Romans 8:17

In my years of studying the Bible, Romans 8:17 has been a touchstone of promise for me. When I realized what it really says, it upended my whole theological belief system regarding inheritance. Let's read this magnificent verse and see exactly what it says.

> *And if children, then heirs; heirs of God, and joint-heirs with Christ; if so be that we suffer with him, that we may be also glorified together.*
> *Romans 8:17*

The first part of this verse clearly states that all children of God are heirs of God. This gives all children of God the promise of eternal life in the new heavens and earth. When I teach this material in classes, I emphasize the reality of it and want to take the opportunity to do so now. If you are a believer in Jesus, you are a child of God and have the gift of eternal life given to you by grace. You are an heir of God and will never lose this standing with the Father.

The verse does not stop with the truth of being an heir of God the Father; it then proceeds to cover being a joint-heir with Christ. As I also do in the classes I teach, let me take the time to ask you a question for which I will demand an answer: Are you a joint-heir with Christ? Most people vehemently declare they are, but then I have them read the rest of the verse. It says you are a joint-heir of Christ if you suffer with Him. The context then concludes that if you suffer with Him, you will be glorified also. Verse 18 continues to say that the sufferings of this present time are not worthy to be compared to the glory that will be revealed in us. (See chapter 5, "The Sufferings and the Glory of the Lord.")

To become a joint-heir with Christ you must suffer with him. (See also chapter 8, "Reigning with the Lord.") We cannot categorically assert that we are joint-heirs with Christ now; we must wait and see what we receive at the judgment seat of Christ.

Children and Sons

There is another qualification to the inheritances of the kingdom of the Father and the kingdom of the Son found in the biblical usages of the words "children" and "sons" (or "daughters").

"Child" is the Greek word *teknon* and means "one who is dearly loved of the Father." "Son" is *huios* and means "a mature child." This nomenclature conveys the difference between a believer and a disciple—one who just accepts Jesus as their Savior, versus one who receives Him as Savior and Lord.

Having just seen that children are heirs of God from Romans 8:17, we can deduce that spiritual children can grow into sons or daughters and become workers as they mature and are about the "family business." This gives us a simple parallel that communicates readily to us. Children are beloved of their father, but as far as working around the house, they are often more of a liability than an asset. But when a child matures into a son or daughter, they can begin taking on more adult responsibilities.

God is equitable in His judgment. If you labor in the family business, you will be rewarded with the revenues coming from it; if you remain a child and do not work, you will still obtain the inheritance that all the children get, but not the revenue of the family business.

To illustrate this, imagine the following: A man and his wife operated a trucking company as a family business. They labored to build the business and became quite successful. In the course of their marriage, they had three children. They loved all of them equally, provided for each of them, and helped to educate them to enter the professional world. The first-born son became a doctor; the second-born child (a daughter) became a lawyer; the third-born (another son), after graduating from business college, returned to work in the family business. Because of his efforts, the business grew tremendously and became more and more profitable.

When the father and mother retired, they liquidated all their assets and gave each of the three children an inheritance. Their assets were $900,000, so each of the children got $300,000, but the son, who worked in the family business, also got the business. Would you have any problem with that?

That story illustrates how God has reserved judgment for His children. All of the kids will get an equal share of His inheritance. They get that because they were born into the family. But the one who works in the family business also gets the inheritance of the business.

There are two inheritances—one is by grace and the other is by merit or reward. If you labor in service, there is granted a reward of the kingdom of the Son; if you do not work, you will receive the inheritance of grace from the Father, but not the inheritance of reward.

Now that we have seen the two inheritances and the two kingdoms explained, the following table will summarize the truths we have discovered.

Inheritances of the Kingdoms

Inheritance of the New Heavens and Earth	Inheritance of the Millennial Kingdom
Salvation of the spirit	Salvation of the soul
Kingdom of the Father (Matthew 13:43)	Kingdom of the Son (Colossians 1:13)
Inheritance of a child (Romans 8:17)	Inheritance of a son (Romans 8:17)
By grace (Titus 3:7; Ephesians 2:8)	By obedience to the Word of God (James 1:21)
Accomplished reality for a Christian	Presently being accomplished by a Christian
Achieved by believing (John 3:16)	Achieved by repenting (Matthew 3:2, 4:17)
Cannot be lost (1 Peter 1:4)	Can be lost (Proverbs 14:14; 2 John 8)
Specific to the gospel of John	Specific to the gospel of Matthew
Milk of the Word of God (Hebrews 5:13)	Meat of the Word of God (Hebrews 5:14)

CHAPTER 7
THE BRIDE COMES OUT OF THE BODY

Another misconception that has resulted from failing to understand our inheritances relates to distinctions between the bride of Christ and the body of Christ. In teachings and songs, these terms are freely interchanged and transposed at the whim of the user. When this is done, the great revelation of Jesus' 1,000-year reign coming to the earth is suppressed.

A succinct statement describing the difference between these two concepts is: *The bride of Christ comes **out of** the body of Christ.* The perfect profile and prototype of this truth was Eve coming out of the body of Adam. The scriptural correlation of these two realities is so overwhelmingly strong that it is clearly God the Father's wish and desire that we know it.

Before documenting this revelation from Ephesians and Genesis, we need to grasp something about the fulfillment of Christ's bride: *This is the great romance in the Word of God.* The Bible reveals God's full complement of emotions from gladness to wrath, but without an understanding of His romance with the bride, the entire character of God is not seen. Jesus, as the manifestation of the Father in the flesh, is

The Bride Comes Out of the Body

a passionate lover who will not be denied His love and His queen. She is the reigning counterpart with Jesus.

The Word of God written in the heavens has Cephas, the King, and Cassiopeia, the Queen, enthroned together.[1] Day unto day and night unto night (Psalm 19) they utter this to the world and have been doing so since the creation of the world. The Song of Solomon depicts the romance the Lord has for His bride, and Hosea 2:16–20 prophesies the recovered covenant of rulership the Lord will have with her in "that day" of 1,000 years. The reason Jesus was not married during His first coming to earth is that the King has arranged His wedding (Matthew 22) to be fulfilled at His second coming. This great romance in the Word of God has a magnificently happy ending.

Now that we have had our romantic passions stirred, we will return to the Word of God to validate this awesome truth. It comes from lofty places in the Word of God—Genesis, the beginning truths, and Ephesians, a pinnacle of revelation in the new covenant.

Genesis 2:24 and Ephesians 5:31

In Ephesians 5, clarion truths and practical principles of marriage are clearly laid out. We see submission, sacrifice, love, and obedience culminating with a direct quote from Genesis 2:24. The purpose behind Genesis 2:24 being quoted in Ephesians 5:31 holds our key to unraveling the mystery of the marriage of the Lord Jesus Christ to His chosen queen.

> *For this cause shall a man leave his father and mother, and shall be joined unto his wife, and they two shall be one flesh.*   *Ephesians 5:31*

In Genesis 2:21 and following, we find a number of salient truths. We see that God caused a deep sleep to fall upon Adam, and while he was sleeping, God took a part out of Adam to make his wife and bride. Since Jesus is referred to as the second Adam (1 Corinthians 15:45–47), there is an obvious parallel within these verses. Just as Eve was taken out of Adam's body, so these verses indicate that the selection of Jesus' bride comes out of His body. This is a type, which prefigures the body of Christ being gathered together off the face of the earth and being asleep to the history of the world, while the bride is chosen out from among the body of Christ.

Genesis 2:23 NKJ plainly states that Adam said, "This is now bone of my bones and flesh of my flesh; she shall be called Woman, because she was taken out of Man." The record then continues in verse 24 with, "Therefore a man shall leave his father and mother and be joined to his wife, and they shall become one flesh." When we see what Ephesians 5:30–32 has been saying to the church, we will realize just how deeply hidden this mystery concerning the reign of the bride with the bridegroom has been.

Ephesians 5:32 proclaims these truths are a great mystery and, like all mysteries—whether they are romance or murder mysteries—this one needs to be solved. Likewise, the culmination of the mystery holds the crescendo of the story line. In the end, those who have been faithful to their Lover will reign with Him in His kingdom. The unfaithful ones will cry and weep when they see what they could have had if they had not left their first love (Revelation 2:4).

Ephesians 5:30 holds the key that will unlock this mystery, but we must do a little detective work to solve the mystery.

> *For we are members of His body, of His flesh and of His bones.*   Ephesians 5:30 NKJ

This seems simple enough on the surface, but there are words missing from the English translation of this verse. The Greek word *ek* is used in the prepositional phrases "of his flesh" and "of his bones." If this word is left out, it implies that the flesh and bones of the body of Christ are what compose the body. This is not what the verse is saying. It is revealing the mystery of the selection of the bride of Christ, because the word *ek* means "out from." Look at the Greek text provided here. I have highlighted *ek* to make it easy to see how this verse should be translated.

> οτι μελη εσμεν του σωματο αυτου **εκ** της σαρκος αυτου και **εκ** των οστεων αυτου
> *Ephesians 5:30*

The proper translation should be "we are members of His body, [coming] out of His flesh and out of His bones." Just as Eve came out from the flesh of Adam (as God opened up the flesh) and out of his bone (the rib), so will the bride of Christ come out of the body of Christ—out of His flesh and out of His bone.

As we go deeper into this "coming out" of the bride of Christ from His body, we will find that many are called, but few are chosen. This phrase is taken directly from Matthew 22—the prophetic picture of the marriage the King arranged for His Son.

Matthew 22

Matthew 22 contains a parable that Jesus spoke concerning the kingdom of heaven. It is one of the most convincing sections of Scripture in the whole Bible dealing with the choosing of the bride of Christ, her reign with the Lord, and what happens to those who will not be chosen. (We will see in chapter 15, "The Outer Darkness," what consequence awaits those who are not chosen.) Suffice it to say for the present that there will be a choosing, because in verse 14 it says, "Many are called, but few are chosen."

This parable pertains to the kingdom of heaven, or as appendix B shows, the reign of the King from heaven on earth. The king (representing God the Father) is arranging a marriage for his son (Jesus the Messiah). The invitations are issued for the wedding, but the first invitees (Israel) did not come. In fact, they killed the servants (the Old Testament prophets, and especially John the Baptist) who announced the wedding. This angered the king (verse 7), and he had the murderers' city burned (which actually happened in A.D. 70 at the hands of General Titus with the Roman Legions).

The king then dispatched a new set of servants (New Testament prophets) to invite any and all that would come (verse 9). When all the guests arrived, there were "both good and bad." The king noticed a man who did not have on a wedding garment (Revelation 19:7–9 further discloses the meaning of this garment) and told his servants to bind him and cast him into the outer darkness. The last verse of this parable tells us that many are called (to the wedding), but few are chosen (to stay and be part of it).

The interpretation of the parable is clear. The whole church of Jesus Christ is called to the marriage supper of the Lamb. Actually, the word "called" (or "bidden" or "invited") forms the root word of "church." ("Church" is *ekklesia* and "call" is *kaleo*.) Those who are called will be judged at the judgment seat of Christ (see chapter 9) to see if they are worthy to reign with the Lord. If they do not have works worthy of the judgment, they will be expelled from the wedding and the 1,000-year reign of the Lord. It is sobering when we realize the Bible says many are called, but few are chosen. How many will be chosen is not known, but the choice of words used does imply that more will miss it than make it.

The conclusive truth emerging out of this parable of the marriage supper of the Lamb in Matthew 22 does not focus on the quality of wine that will be served, or who the best man will be (but my guess is John the Baptist), or the fame of the band that will play the wedding march. The stated emphasis is that many are called, but few will be chosen. We need to have our wedding garments on if we want to reign with the Lord in His 1,000-year kingdom.

The Wedding Garment

Revelation 19:7–9 gives us a definition of the wedding garment. The scope and context of the event is the same as Matthew 22—the marriage supper of the Lamb.

> *"Let us be glad and rejoice and give Him glory, for the marriage of the Lamb has come, and His wife has made herself ready." And to her it was granted to be arrayed in fine linen, clean and bright, for the fine linen is the righteous acts of the saints. Then he said to me, "Write: 'Blessed are those who are called to the marriage supper of the Lamb!'" And he said to me, "These are the true sayings of God."*
> *Revelation 19:7–9 NKJ*

These verses will lay the foundation for the next section in our study, "Entering the Kingdom," by revealing the necessary preparation to receive our wedding attire. Verse 7 says that the wife makes herself ready. This is not a gift of grace, but it is one of merit. According to verse 8, the fine linen is "the righteous acts of the saints." We see from this verse that it is not just any kind of works, but righteous acts. These are works built upon the grace of God that contribute to building the kingdom upon the earth.

Also notice that verse 9 says that these are the true sayings of God. In other words, the testimony of the Word of God concerning this aspect of revelation is that it is absolutely true. There will be a choosing of the bride out of the body of Christ and the criterion for being chosen will be laboring to build the kingdom while living on earth. This is the reward of inheritance.

The Example of Rebekah

Another type for the bride of Christ involves the selection of a bride for Isaac. This account comes from

Genesis 24. Again, there are figures that will pattern the story.

Abraham, the father, wanted to choose a bride for his son, Isaac. Isaac was the son of promise, and Abraham, who believed in arranged marriages, wanted to qualify the bride. (This is done even today in some countries, i.e., India.) In this record, Isaac represents Jesus Christ and Rebekah, who was chosen, represents His bride.

The servant who was sent to select the bride was Eliezer. The name Eliezer means "God who helps," and it is the Holy Spirit who is our Helper. Here is a clear representation of the Holy Spirit.

First, the father (God or Abraham) arranged the marriage for the son (Jesus or Isaac). He sent his servant (the Holy Spirit or Eliezer) to choose the bride out from a select group. Abraham sent Eliezer to the daughter of his people in Mesopotamia. Likewise the Holy Spirit was sent to a select group which includes the following: (1) those of Israel who believed on the coming of the Messiah, (2) the church of the body of Christ, and (3) those who will embrace Jesus as Messiah during the great tribulation.

Abraham made Eliezer swear to bring the chosen bride back to him; likewise, the Holy Spirit will bring back to the Father the selected ones from the earth.

Eliezer found Rebekah willing to work and not just sit idly and be beautiful. Part of Rebekah's qualifications was that she had to be willing to work, just the same as those who are chosen out of the church.

I have heard of a book entitled, *The Bride of Christ Wears Combat Boots*. This title is derived from Revelation 19:11–14, which indicates that the bride also makes up the army that is dressed in white and coming with the Lord. Additionally, the bride of Christ wears work boots. God is not looking for a lazy woman to sit around and be fanned with a palm leaf. The

The Bride Comes Out of the Body

bride of Christ who will receive the reward of inheritance will be chosen according to her works—her own righteous acts.

Hosea 2:16–20

The covenant the Lord will enter into with His bride is stated in Hosea 2:16–20. The theme of Hosea is God's forgiveness toward Israel, His beloved. He reveals this by telling Hosea to marry a harlot, so the prophet would understand how God felt about Israel. The Lord is saying in chapter 2, verses 16 through 20 that He will forgive those who love Him and betroth them to Him in the day of the Lord (the 1,000-year reign).

> *"And it shall be, in that day [the day that lasts 1,000 years]," says the LORD, "That you will call Me 'My Husband,' and no longer call Me 'My Master,' For I will take from her mouth the names of the Baals, and they shall be remembered by their name no more. In that day I will make a covenant for them with the beasts of the field, with the birds of the air, and with the creeping things of the ground. Bow and sword of battle I will shatter from the earth, to make them lie down safely. I will betroth you to Me forever; yes, I will betroth you to Me in righteousness and justice, in lovingkindness and mercy; I will betroth you to Me in faithfulness, and you shall know the LORD."*   Hosea 2:16–20 NKJ

The covenant of rulership will be very similar to the one initially made with Adam. This will be rulership with Jesus Christ in the millennial reign, as God had originally intended it to be with Adam.

In summary, there is a reward of inheritance given to those who faithfully serve their first love and work in the kingdom business while living on earth. The body of Christ is called by grace, but the bride is chosen out from the body based upon the criterion of being worthy of reigning with the Lord in the 1,000-year kingdom that is coming on the earth.

We will see more of the requirements that must be met in order to be included in the millennial kingdom in the next chapter, "Reigning with the Lord."

CHAPTER 8
Reigning with the Lord

There is a section of Scripture found in 2 Timothy 2 that summarizes both the inheritances of grace and reward. These verses were a hallmark of faith and an anchor of truth to the first-century believers in Christ.

> *It is a faithful saying: For if we be dead with him, we shall also live with him: If we suffer, we shall also reign with him: if we deny him, he also will deny us: If we believe not, yet he abideth faithful: he cannot deny himself.*
> *2 Timothy 2:11–13*

It is commonly believed by Bible scholars that these verses were in fact a song that believers sang in the early church. They are even indented in the New King James Version and set apart as a separate section. It is easy to see how this could have been a song. I can imagine the believers singing this song and having it remind them of the millennial kingdom that would come to the earth. I believe it gave them strength to stand in their difficult times, just as it does for us today.

We will closely examine these verses to find the criteria for reigning with the Lord in the 1,000-year period. Before we do this, we should look at some scriptures that document the subject of reigning with the Lord during this time period.

> *And hast made us unto our God kings and priests: and we shall reign on the earth.*
> *Revelation 5:10*

> *And the seventh angel sounded; and there were great voices in heaven, saying, The kingdoms of this world are become the kingdoms of our Lord, and of his Christ; and he shall reign for ever and ever.*
> *Revelation 11:15*

> *And I saw thrones, and they sat upon them, and judgment was given unto them: and I saw the souls of them that were beheaded for the witness of Jesus, and for the word of God, and which had not worshipped the beast, neither his image, neither had received his mark upon their foreheads, or in their hands; and they lived and reigned with Christ a thousand years.*
> *Revelation 20:4*

> *Blessed and holy is he that hath part in the first resurrection: on such the second death hath no power, but they shall be priests of God and of Christ, and shall reign with him a thousand years.*
> *Revelation 20:6*

In addition to these verses, there are others that specify rulership during the millennial kingdom.

> *His lord said unto him, Well done, thou good and faithful servant: thou hast been faithful over a few things, I will make thee ruler over many things: enter thou into the joy of thy lord.*
> *Matthew 25:21*

> *And he said unto him, Well done, thou good servant: because thou hast been faithful in a very little, have thou authority over ten cities.*
> *Luke 19:17*

These verses leave no doubt that a literal truth of a 1,000-year reign with Jesus on the earth will someday exist. Whoever these individuals are, there is no doubt according to biblical accuracy that they will live and that this reign shall absolutely transpire. Someone is going to rule with the Lord Jesus—why not you?

Second Timothy 2:11–13 demonstrate a very interesting structure. Verses 11 and 13 reveal the inheritance of grace, and verse 12 shows the inheritance of reward.

> *This is a faithful saying: For if we died with Him, we shall also live with Him.*
> *2 Timothy 2:11 NKJ*

The indication that this may have been a hymn sung by the early church is the phrase, "This is a faithful saying." The concept of, "if we died with Him [Christ]" was used by the Apostle Paul in Romans 6:6 and 8, Galatians 2:20, and Colossians 3:3 to show that the old man died and we are already a new creation in Christ Jesus (also see 2 Corinthians 5:17).

We died with the Lord when He was crucified; the promise is that we shall live with Him in the new heavens and earth. When 2 Timothy 2:11 says that we also shall live with Him, it emphasizes the absoluteness of the statement even above the future tense of the verb. This is the promise of grace.

Verse 13 also refers to the inheritance of grace when it says, "He cannot deny Himself."

> *If we are faithless, He remains faithful; He cannot deny Himself.*
> *2 Timothy 2:13 NKJ*

According to James 2:17, faith without works is dead. Therefore, this verse means that if we or anyone else does not work, God still cannot deny the promise of the new heavens and earth that will come to all of His children. He cannot deny Himself, because He made the promise and God cannot lie (Titus 1:2; Hebrews 6:18).

This brings us to the sandwich verse that reveals the millennial kingdom and the inheritance of works or reward.

> *If we suffer, we shall also reign with him: if we deny him, he also will deny us.*
>
> *2 Timothy 2:12*

There is a necessary distinction to be drawn between verses 12 and 13 on the subject of denying. There is a difference between the kingdoms of the Father and the Son, and the inheritance of grace and reward. If you deny Jesus, He will deny you at the judgment seat of Christ; however, if you do not do any works, the Father will still accept you into the kingdom of the Father.

We are still endeavoring to show the criteria for reigning with Jesus. From verse 12, we see that to reign with Him we must suffer with Him. This brings us back to chapter 6, "The Inheritances of Grace and Reward," where we looked at Romans 8:17 and 18. If we want to be joint-heirs with Christ and to reign with Him in His kingdom, we must suffer with Him. The sufferings we experience, according to Romans 8:18, are not worthy to be compared to the glory that we shall receive with Him. Life in the millennial reign will certainly be glorious, but we cannot deny Him if we want it.

If someone holds a pistol to your head and says, "Deny Christ!" you would be a fool to do so. Those who deny Him forfeit their ticket into the millennial kingdom.

This topic reminds me of a story I once heard. During times of persecution in China, ten families were lined up with father, mother, and children being threatened with death. As the executioner dealt with each family, the children and then the mother were shot if the father would not deny Jesus. When it came to one specific couple, the executioner held the gun to the temple of their child and demanded that the father deny Jesus. He did not and the child was murdered on the spot. When the gun was put to his wife's head, the father began to waiver in his commitment. His wife had the right response. She said, "Husband, if you deny the Lord, we may live but we will still eat slop with the pigs tonight; but if you do not deny Jesus, we will dine with Him tonight."

Matthew 10:24 says that the servant is not above his master. Jesus suffered—will you? He was truly faithful till the end, and Revelation 2:10 says if you are faithful unto death you will receive a crown of life. You must be faithful all the days of your life and never deny Him. That is why the denials of Peter were so grave. Peter denied Jesus three times (Matthew 26) and Jesus later made Peter confess his love for Him three times (John 21). If you deny Jesus, He will deny you (entrance to His kingdom on earth) at His judgment seat.

In conclusion of this section on "Understanding Our Inheritances," we must remember that we already have the inheritance of the new heavens and earth. It is the gift of eternal life that came by grace and can never be lost. It is incorruptible and fades not away (1 Peter 1:3–4). In contrast, the inheritance of reward is given to those who faithfully serve in the family business.

The bride of Christ will come out of the body of Christ, just as Eve came out of Adam. Many are called into the church by grace and will have the opportunity to display their righteous acts at the marriage supper of the Lamb. Many are called but few will be chosen.

Those individuals who suffer with the Lord will reign with Him. Those who deny Him will miss the kingdom reserved for those who have proven themselves worthy. We did die with Him, being buried by baptism with Him unto death; so shall we live with Him. Even if we are faithless, we will still gain entrance into the new heavens and earth. Better still, the Lord wants you to reign with Him. That is why the Holy Spirit has come—to help you prepare for the judgment seat of Christ, where we will all have our works displayed to see if we are worthy to rule with the Lord in His 1,000-year kingdom.

SECTION THREE
Entering the Kingdom

We have seen that there will indeed be a 1,000-year reign of Jesus on the earth. We now need to deal with the actualities of how to enter this kingdom. In this section we will move all the way from the judgment seat of Christ to the keys for entering the kingdom.

This section will cover the benefits of fulfilling the requirements for being a part of Jesus' 1,000-year reign, and it will show the consequences of not fulfilling them. In order to lay a proper foundation, we will take a look at the benefits of qualifying before covering the consequences of missing the kingdom. (However, you may find it preferential to read the next section on missing the kingdom first in order to leave a positive motivation in your mind at the end of the study.)

The premise of what we will discover and affirm through this section is that all Christians will be judged to discover their worthiness to reign with the Lord. If they are wearing a white wedding garment at the marriage supper of the Lamb, they will be allowed to stay and then return to the earth with the Lord for the 1,000-year reign. If not, they depart into the outer darkness to remain for the duration of that reign. The details concerning the outer darkness will be covered in the next section.

There are some very "meaty" matters in these next chapters, so I encourage you to study to show yourself approved unto God by rightly dividing the word of truth. The proper cutting of the Word of God will mandate a place for this kingdom. It absolutely will come, and each and every one of us will stand before the Lord. I pray that this biblical information better prepares you for that day, so that you may be judged worthy to enter into the kingdom of the Lord Jesus.

CHAPTER 9

THE JUDGMENT SEAT OF CHRIST

As a Christian, wherever you are or whatever you are doing right now, someday you will stand before the Lord Jesus Christ and be judged by Him. He will either say to you, "Well done good and faithful servant; enter into the kingdom," or "You wicked and slothful servant; enter into the outer darkness." One place will be bliss; the other place will be bleak. At the judgment seat of Christ, you will be judged and either rewarded or punished. God has spoken in His Word and He is incapable of lying (Hebrews 6:17–19). You *will* appear there someday.

Many times the subject of the judgment seat of Christ gets buried under the rubble of "rapture discussion." We relegate the actuality of the judgment seat to a place of secondary importance behind the timing of it. Not so here. We are not discussing *when* the Lord is returning to gather His church, but *what* will happen when He does. Whether the church is taken off the earth before, during, or after the great tribulation, we will all appear before the judgment seat of Christ. Whether you are a Messianic Jew, a Protestant, or a Roman Catholic, you will be judged for what you have done on the earth during your life. We will all go to the judgment seat of Christ.

> *For **we must all appear before the judgment seat of Christ**; that every one may receive the things done in his body, according to that he hath done, whether it be good or bad.*   2 Corinthians 5:10

Notice that this verse says that there will be a judgment of whether the works were bad or good. This contradicts the teachings floating around the body of Christ that this judgment of the Lord is only for rewards. I have heard teachings that this is the *bema* judgment and indicates the place where Olympians were awarded garlands for their victories. Although this sounds very positive and spiritual, unfortunately, it is not scriptural. The word *bema* also describes the place of judgment for punishment as well.

> *Then all the Greeks took Sosthenes, the chief ruler of the synagogue, and beat him before the judgment seat [bema]. And Gallio cared for none of those things.*   Acts 18:17

People sometimes adopt this theory when seeking a belief system to excuse sin and refute punishment for wrongdoing. This reminds me of a cartoon I recently saw. Three men were descending into the flames of hell on an escalator. One looked at the other two and said, "You have nothing to worry about. Our board of elders voted 3 to 5 last week that this place does not exist." The same scenario applies here, too. You can believe what you want to, and try to dismiss the fact that judgment is coming, but it will not negate the truth that it will come.

Notice what 2 Corinthians 5:11 says.

> *Knowing therefore the terror of the Lord, we persuade men; but we are made manifest unto God; and I trust also are made manifest in your consciences.*   2 Corinthians 5:11

The Judgment Seat of Christ

If the *bema* were only a seat for reward, then why bring up the terror of the Lord? No, this is a place where the books will be opened and your account will be read.

> *But why dost thou judge thy brother? or why dost thou set at nought thy brother? for we shall all stand before the judgment seat of Christ. For it is written, As I live, saith the Lord, every knee shall bow to me, and every tongue shall confess to God. So then every one of us shall give account of himself to God.*
>
> *Romans 14:10–12*

The word for "account" is the Greek word *logon*, which actually means the same as a bank account where deposits and withdrawals are made. We are making entries daily by the works that we do. Some day, the books will be opened and we will give account of the things we have done, whether good or bad.

My good friend, Lonnell Johnson, has written a poem, based upon a quotation by Elijah Pierce, about the kind of book each life is writing. This poem is quoted from the book, *Stone Upon Stone: Psalms of Remembrance*.

Your Life Is a Book

> "Your life is a book, and everyday is a page. You cannot deny the pages of your own book, because you've already written into the pages of life. And that life will be open in the eyes of God. When the book is finished, you cannot deny it."   Elijah Pierce

Your life is a book, and everyday is a page.
We all write our life story, whether as fool or sage.

> Printed words in boldface type impress to curse
>   or bless,
> Revealing a full measure of failure or success
> In applying our hearts unto wisdom as we age.
>
> No one knows the future nor can anyone gauge
> The impact of a solitary life with its message.
> Each word of our history continues to stress
> Your life is a book.
>
> Work heartily as to the Lord, no matter the wage.
> Accept this, for it is futile to wrestle and rage
> Against God's divine plan that we might know Him
>   and express
> His purpose, daily striving to write as we progress.
> From infant to elder, through each unfolding stage,
> Your life is a book.

The concept of giving an account, "whether it be good or bad," is also covered in Colossians 3:25, which refers to the "reward of the inheritance."

> *Knowing that of the Lord ye shall receive the reward of the inheritance: for ye serve the Lord Christ. But he that doeth wrong shall receive for the wrong which he hath done: and there is no respect of persons.*
> *Colossians 3:24–25*

This verse of scripture is an anchor point of revelation concerning the two different inheritances. Now we shall look at the rewards aspect of the inheritance.

Rewards of the Inheritance

First Corinthians 3 provides valuable detail concerning rewards in the 1,000-year kingdom and the qualifications for works that will earn them. As the teaching in this chapter develops, the aspect of judgment and the judgment seat of Christ will arise. The context begins in verse 8.

> *Now he that planteth and he that watereth are one: and every man shall receive his own reward according to his own labour.*
> *1 Corinthians 3:8*

This verse documents that each one will be rewarded for the labor they have done. Verses 10 and 11 introduce the metaphor of a building and its foundation representing the foundation of the Lord Jesus Christ that we must all build upon. No other work will pass the test in order for rewards to be administered. Verse 12 shows that there are different works and that each one will be rewarded according to the value of their work. Verse 13 gets straight to the matter of judgment.

> *Every man's work shall be made manifest: for the day shall declare it, because it shall be revealed by fire; and the fire shall try every man's work of what sort it is.*
> *1 Corinthians 3:13*

The day when works will be judged to see if rewards are merited is the day of the judgment seat of Christ. At that time and before the Lord, fire will test the works. If the physical substance burns, no reward will be given, but if the substance is burned and residual blessings remain, then those works will have passed the test of fire.

Revelation 11:14–18 provides details concerning the judgment of rewards. Although I am not going into depth in these verses, it appears that loud voices in heaven and the 24 elders are prophetically proclaiming the coming events of Christ's kingdom and the judgment seat of Christ. These proclamations are interesting in that they happen between the second and third woe, just after the resurrection and ascension of the two witnesses and just before the coming of the antichrist. Notice that rewards will be given to the prophets and saints who have feared the Lord.

> *And the nations were angry, and thy wrath is come, and the time of the dead, that they should be judged, and that thou shouldest give reward unto thy servants the prophets, and to the saints, and them that fear thy name, small and great; and shouldest destroy them which destroy the earth.* Revelation 11:18

We have mentioned Revelation 20:4 in the assertion of a 1,000-year reign, but look also at the reward given to those in the kingdom. A significant aspect of their reward will be to rule and reign with the Lord Himself.

> *And I saw thrones, and they sat upon them, and judgment was given unto them: and I saw the souls of them that were beheaded for the witness of Jesus, and for the word of God, and which had not worshipped the beast, neither his image, neither had received his mark upon their foreheads, or in their hands; and they lived and reigned with Christ a thousand years.* Revelation 20:4

Those who sit on thrones will be kings and lords. That is why Jesus will be King of kings and Lord of lords. Kings and lords will wear crowns. There are four places that reveal the kinds of crowns available to those who labor in the family business. They are the crown of rejoicing (1 Thessalonians 2:19), the crown of righteousness (2 Timothy 4:8), the crown of glory (1 Peter 5:4), and the crown of life (James 1:12).

Again, my emphasis is not to debate the timing of the judgment seat of Christ, but to emphatically demonstrate that it does indeed exist and that rewards will be given from it to those who serve the Lord. Second John also indicates it is necessary to labor to receive our rewards.

> *Look to yourselves, that we lose not those things which we have wrought, but that we receive a full reward.*   2 John 8

To strive for the masteries requires individual diligence from each of us. Our fate is in our own hands, and how we are judged at the judgment seat of Christ will be determined by the works and righteous acts we each perform in this life now.

As we continue in our study, we will focus on the reward of the inheritance that will await those of us who labor in the family business.

CHAPTER 10
THE OUT RESURRECTION

In our last chapter we established that rewards will be given at the judgment seat of Christ. In this chapter, we will find that one of the greatest rewards to be given for the millennial reign is a body in which to live.

We are going to textually examine Philippians 3:10–21 to uncover this great teaching about the *out resurrection* and the new body that will be given to those who press for the upward calling of God in Christ Jesus. People have read this section of the Word of God for years and skipped over the portion where the great Apostle Paul says, "If by any means I might attain unto the resurrection of the dead." We will discover what this entails and see that the context of this entire section is the 1,000-year reign of Jesus on the earth.

Philippians 3:10–21

The context of these verses begins with the Apostle Paul saying that he counted all things loss that he might gain Christ and be found in Him.

> *And be found in him, not having mine own righteousness, which is of the law, but that*

> *which is through the faith of Christ, the righteousness which is of God by faith: That I may know him, and the power of his resurrection, and the fellowship of his sufferings, being made conformable unto his death.*   *Philippians 3:9–10*

From Romans 8:17 and 18 we have already seen that becoming a joint-heir with Christ is the reward awaiting those who share in His sufferings. This is also what Philippians 3:10 is saying. The next verse has puzzled Bible scholars for years.

> *If by any means I might attain unto the resurrection of the dead.*
> *Philippians 3:11*

Notice the word "if." This passage certainly cannot mean that the Apostle Paul was not sure if he was born again or not. It is saying that *if* Paul suffered with the Lord, he might attain (receive) this "resurrection." Deepening our understanding of this word will clarify and explain this whole section of Philippians 3.

The word usually translated as "resurrection" is *anastasis*. This *anastasis*, or resurrection, is a root word with a prefix. *Stasis* means "to stand" and *ana* means "to do something again." So, resurrection literally means *to stand again*. The Old Testament contains a metaphor that exemplifies this truth as Ezekiel (37:4–10) prophesied to dry bones, and they stood again.

The word "resurrection" in Philippians 3:11 is the Greek word *exanastasis*. This is the only usage of this word in the Bible. *Exanastasis* has an extra prefix that reveals exactly what Paul was saying and gives this word its unique meaning and understanding concerning the 1,000-year reign. *Ex*, or *ek*, means "out from." So what *exanastasis* means is that there is a coming "out from among those who stand or rise again." It is an out resurrection, or a coming out from among those who have been raised from the dead. This is what will happen for those who are judged worthy of Jesus' 1,000-year reign. They will come out from among the raised dead in Christ and will enter into glory with the Lord on the earth.

We read earlier in Matthew 22:14 that "many are called, but few are chosen." Philippians 3:11 is the complement to that truth. All the called of Jesus Christ will be raised from the dead and go to the judgment seat of Christ. Coming out from among those will be the chosen who will inherit the kingdom of the Lord Jesus Christ. Those who are not chosen will still inherit the kingdom of the Father, but will have to wait out the 1,000 years while the Lord and His bride establish His kingdom on the earth.

This is what the Apostle Paul meant when he said, "*If* I attain unto the *out resurrection* [emphasis added]." He was striving to gain it, just like you and me. He was saying (in my words), "I know that I am saved, but I am still striving for the reward of inheritance that I might be chosen to reign with Him for whom I have suffered." Now look at the next verse.

> *Not as though I had already attained [received], either were already perfect [totally mature]: but I follow [chase] after, if that I may apprehend [get] that for which also I am apprehended [gotten] of Christ Jesus.*   *Philippians 3:12*

Paul realized that he had to finish what he had started and that if he quit in the process he would disqualify himself from the competition.

> *Brethren, I count not myself to have apprehended [received the prize]: but this one thing I do, forgetting those things which are*

> behind, and reaching forth unto those things which are before. *Philippians 3:13*

Then comes the popular verse of pressing "toward the mark of the prize."

> *I press toward [or having the motion of continuing toward] the mark for the prize [of the kingdom] of the high calling of God in Christ Jesus.* *Philippians 3:14*

"Press" is an active word that is translated "persecute" in many places. Its literal meaning is "to pursue" or "to follow hard after," and it gives the implication that we must push with everything we have if we are going to gain the prize of the millennial reign with the Lord.

> *Let us therefore, as many as be perfect [mature], be thus minded [to press]: and if in any thing ye be otherwise minded [to back off and get lazy] God shall reveal even this unto you.* *Philippians 3:15*

God sent the Holy Spirit as our Helper to get us into the kingdom. God the Father, Jesus the Son, and the Holy Spirit all want us in the kingdom of heaven (Luke 12:32), but we have the responsibility of pressing in and following the lead of the Holy Spirit.

> *Nevertheless, whereto we have already attained [gained], let us [continue to] walk by the same rule, let us mind [stay mindful of] the same thing.* *Philippians 3:16*

This is why Galatians 6:9 says, "And let us not be weary in well doing: for in due season we shall reap, if we faint not."

> *Brethren, be followers [imitators] together of me, and mark [skopeo—to fix your eyes and*

> *attention upon] them which walk so as ye have us for an ensample.   Philippians 3:17*

We are to pay attention to those individuals who are striving for the masteries and use them as examples, as opposed to the individuals Paul talks about in the next two verses. Watch the parenthesis—it is referring to those who do not make the millennial reign.

> *(For many walk, of whom I have told you often, and now tell you even weeping, that they are the enemies of the cross of Christ: whose end is destruction, whose god is their belly, and whose glory is in their shame, who mind earthly things.)   Philippians 3:18–19*

People who are called and born again sometimes become enemies of the cross by their example of following after the things of the world.

"Destruction" is the Greek word *apoleia*. The root *olethropos* means "ruin" and the prefix *apo* means "to be separated." Literally, this word describes the separation of people in the outer darkness during the millennial reign. They are separated away from the light and therefore are in outer darkness. It happens because they follow their own desires (bellies) instead of doing the commandments of the Lord. Their glory is their own, not the Lord's, and they are attentive to earthly, not heavenly things.

Now we will see the conclusion of those chosen to be part of the out resurrection. Verse 20 is frequently used at funeral services and proclaimed as a promise to those who are born again. This promise will be given to those who are chosen, not just called. This may cut across theological lines, but the whole context of Philippians 3:10–21 cannot be denied. This is not just talking about individuals who are born again, but those who are pressing in for the prize of the millennial reign.

The Out Resurrection

> *For our conversation [citizenship] is in heaven; from whence also we look for the Saviour, the Lord Jesus Christ.*
> *Philippians 3:20*

All Christians have a promised citizenship in heaven, and we all look for the Savior to come and gather us off the planet, but only those who mind heavenly things will receive a glorious body like the Lord's enabling them to reign with Him on the earth.

> *Who shall change our vile body, that it may be fashioned like unto his glorious body, according to the working whereby he is able even to subdue all things unto himself.*
> *Philippians 3:21*

It is an erroneous deduction to think that just because you are saved, you will receive a glorious body to live and reign in during the millennial kingdom. Notice that verse 21 says that the glorious body is fashioned like unto His, according to the standard of subduing all things. Subduing all things unto Himself is His responsibility in the millennial kingdom (1 Corinthians 15:24). This again emphasizes that glorious bodies will be given to those individuals who will reign with the Lord on the earth. Upon dying or being gathered to the Lord, we will all appear before the judgment seat of Christ to receive for the things we have done. If you are among the chosen, you will be given a glorious body to reign with the Lord on the earth.

Those individuals who are called but not chosen will not need a physical body fashioned like unto the Lord's because they will not be upon the earth, but in the outer darkness weeping and gnashing their teeth (because they are sad or mad that they did not make the millennial kingdom).

The 1,000 Year Reign of Jesus Christ on the Earth

We will either enjoy the reign on the earth with Jesus, or endure separation from Him in the outer darkness during that time. In our next chapter, "The Good and Faithful Servant," we will continue to see the standards we must apply in order to enter the kingdom.

CHAPTER 11
THE GOOD AND FAITHFUL SERVANT

Matthew 25:14–30 gives one of the most clear-cut teachings about the benefit of the kingdom and the consequence of the outer darkness found anywhere in the Bible. The earlier parable in Matthew 25 of the wise and foolish virgins teaches the same truth—with those who are prepared going in to the marriage, but the foolish and unprepared ones being shut out. Both passages illustrate that the kingdom of heaven will have people who make it and people who miss it.

The records of the good and faithful servants and the lazy and wicked servant are covered in Matthew 25 and Luke 19. Both accounts say basically the same thing, with the exception that Luke specifically mentions rewards being granted (as rulers over cities). The same lesson emerges out of both parables: good and faithful servants will receive the kingdom, but wicked and lazy servants will be separated into the outer darkness during that time period.

Although these records are reasonably well known, since we are concerned at this point with the judgments made upon the servants, looking at some background will add more light to the subject.

> *For the kingdom of heaven is as a man travelling into a far country, who called his own servants, and delivered unto them his goods. And unto one he gave five talents, to another two, and to another one; to every man according to his several ability; and straightway took his journey.*
> *Matthew 25:14–15*

Note that this parable is dealing with the kingdom of heaven, a specific usage common only to the gospel of Matthew, which depicts Jesus as King. Also it is particularly important to note that talents have been given to each according to his own ability.

Jesus is the great administrator of the church of the body of Christ and is responsible for doling out the talents, ministries and services to His people. He gives people talents commensurate with their abilities. To those with more ability, He gives more talents. Then, according to fairness, to whom much is given, much is required (Luke 12:48). This principle is crucial to remember when we consider the judgment to come upon each and every one of us. Regardless of what you have or the talents you have been given, you must invest everything you have to receive maximum yield on the talent the Lord has given you.

The parable continues with the lord leaving these individuals in charge of the talents he gave them for a season. To one he gave five, to another he gave two, and to another he gave one. Then after awhile, the lord returned to judge them for what he had entrusted to them. The one who had five made five more; the one who had two made two more, and the one who had one hid it in the earth because of fear. Let the lessons begin.

The Good and Faithful Servant

The lord says the identical thing to the ones who made five and two. This shows that there is no respect of persons and to whom much is given, much is required.

> *His lord said unto him, Well done, thou good and faithful servant: thou hast been faithful over a few things, I will make thee ruler over many things: enter thou into the joy of thy lord.*   Matthew 25:21 or 23

Notice that this lord calls his servant "good and faithful." These are the requirements for entering into the kingdom. It matters not how much ability you have or in what position the Lord places you to serve. He requires that you be good and faithful. Many times people say, "I don't know what to do." The Lord would say to them, "Be good and if you do not know what to do, be faithful at being good and I will show you where to go." It is not a coincidence that good comes before faithful.

These two adjectives describe character and work ethic. It is not a matter of either/or, but both/and. Lots of people are good and lots of people are faithful, but the Lord requires both. Character is a matter of having goodness, and faithfulness is a matter of doing consistently. The Lord wants you in the balance of being and doing. Character is being; faithfulness is doing. He will reward you for both of these.

The reward, according to Matthew 25, is to enter into the joy of the Lord, and the description from Luke 19 is rulership over cities. Perhaps the joy will be to rule. I hope to find out along with you.

The plot thickened when the servant to whom one talent was given was quizzed about his affairs.

> *Then he which had received the one talent came and said, Lord, I knew thee that thou art an hard man, reaping where thou*

> *hast not sown, and gathering where thou hast not strawed: And I was afraid, and went and hid thy talent in the earth: lo, there thou hast that is thine.*   *Matthew 25: 24–25*

I have found it interesting that the one to whom less was given was the one who was afraid. It seems as though the greatest trials come upon us when we seemingly have little ability or talent; this is when we are afraid. Nevertheless, it is fear that destroys us—whether it is the fear of losing or the fear of failing, it is fear that will keep any one of us out of the millennial kingdom.

This admonition does not just deal with people in general, but also separate abilities that we may have. For example, I have always liked to sing and was involved in a number of choirs while I was growing up. I currently believe that my abilities in teaching and writing are the dominant abilities that the Lord gave me, but I do not want to hide anything. When I realized this, I began singing at some of the ministry meetings that I have done. Do you know what happened? People began coming to me and saying, "That song really blessed me—not because of the exactness of your performance, but your willingness to do it." Then they would say, "You know, I really have the ministry of music and your willingness to do this has inspired me to be 'good and faithful' with my talents, too."

The lord was very harsh with the man who had only one talent and hid it. In appendix A, I will explain that parables were hidden messages for the church that would arise later. So, church, listen up. If you want to see the harsh side of the Lord, all you have to do is do nothing. Wicked or lazy—either one will work.

> *His lord answered and said unto him, Thou wicked and slothful servant, thou knewest that I reap where I sowed not, and gather where I*

The Good and Faithful Servant

have not strawed: Thou oughtest therefore to have put my money to the exchangers, and then at my coming I should have received mine own with usury.   Matthew 25:26–27

I have mused over how someone could only receive interest on a latent ability and never actually use it. The best guess I can come up with is that the person talks about doing something with it and never does it. The old sayings still apply: "Talk is cheap," and "The road to hell is paved with good intentions."

The conclusion of the matter is that the Lord will take the one talent from the wicked and/or lazy servant and give it to another who has more and will command that the wicked and lazy one be cast into the outer darkness. The teaching on the outer darkness is yet to be covered (in chapter 15), but suffice it to say that it is a real place, and believe me—you do *not* want to go there.

Jesus himself declared the parable which says He is a hard man (Matthew 25:24–26; Luke 19:22 NIV) when it comes to judging. When you stand before Him, He will be seated on the judgment seat, dressed in His kingly robes and functioning in His role as Judge. He will not be holding a shepherd's crook, but a rod of iron and a sword.

We will see in the chapter dealing with keys to entering the kingdom that a major prerequisite to enter the kingdom is repentance. Jesus and John the Baptist both said, "Repent, the kingdom of heaven is at hand." If you have been slothful or wicked, repent now while Jesus is holding the shepherd's crook and is kneeling before the mercy seat making intercession for you. When He stands up and takes His place as Judge, Jesus, according to His own words, will be a harsh man.

Simply stated—repent and change if you have been wicked and slothful. On the other hand, if you have been good and faithful, be not weary in well doing, for in due season you will reap if you faint not.

CHAPTER 12
Laboring to Enter into the Rest

The book of Hebrews is an enigma to many Christians because of its many references to Old Testament concepts and commandments. Chapters 3 and 4 are prime examples, using the children of Israel and their journey to the Promised Land in the past as a comparison to the millennial reign of the Lord that would come in the future.

The children of Israel had to labor to enter into the Promised Land, just as Christians must labor to enter into Jesus' millennial kingdom. Many of the Israelites did not make it and fell by the wayside on the way to their final home. Hebrews 3:17–19 speaks of this.

> *But with whom was he grieved forty years? was it not with them that had sinned, whose carcases fell in the wilderness? And to whom sware he that they should not enter into his rest, but to them that believed not? So we see that they could not enter in because of unbelief.*
> *Hebrews 3:17–19*

Hebrews 3:19 and 4:1 provide us a comparison between the children of Israel and the church today.

> *So we see that they could not enter in because of unbelief. Let us therefore fear, lest, a promise being left us of entering into his rest, any of you should seem to come short of it.*
> *Hebrews 3:19 and 4:1*

There is a rest remaining for the people of God, and His exhortation for us is to labor to enter into that rest.

> *There remaineth therefore a rest to the people of God. Let us labour therefore to enter into that rest, lest any man fall after the same example of unbelief.* *Hebrews 4:9 and 11*

The phrase "labor to enter into that rest" may seem like a contradiction of terms, but actually we all do this in order to take a day off from work. When we go on vacation, we work and work and work ahead so that we will not have to work during our vacation. Christians should be laboring day after day to enter into the rest of the millennial kingdom that is coming.

These lessons from Hebrews 3 and 4 are very impacting. They compare Moses and Jesus, as the heads of the children of Israel and the church, respectively. Then the exhortations and parallels begin. The children of Israel provoked the Lord with the hardness of their hearts (3:8 and 15, 4:7) and, by implication, the church is encouraged not to do the same.

The table on the following page will list some of the underlying analogies that the children of Israel and their journey to the Promised Land hold in relation to the church today.

Old Testament Truth Concealed	New Testament Truth Revealed
Egypt	The world
Pharaoh	Devil
Moses	Jesus Christ
The sea	Water baptism
The cloud	The Holy Spirit
Wilderness	Life
Promised Land	Millennial kingdom
Crossing the Jordan to enter the Promised Land	Judgment seat of Christ

Before coming to the conclusion of Hebrews 3 and 4, it is necessary to discuss the content of Hebrews 4:9–11. Yes, we as the church are laboring to enter into the millennial kingdom, but at the same time, because of Jesus' redemptive accomplishments for us, we are to rest in His accomplishments. Look at the added notes in the verses, and this will become clearer.

> *There remaineth therefore a rest [the millennial kingdom] to the people of God. For he that is entered into his rest [from being justified by his works], he also hath ceased from his own works [of justification], as God did from his [works on the Sabbath].*

> *Let us labour [with works of service] therefore to enter into that rest [of the millennial kingdom], lest any man fall after the same example of unbelief [as the children of Israel when they provoked God through disobedience].* Hebrews 4:9–11

The usage of "rest" for God's people contains one of the best documentations for the millennial kingdom and the week of millennia in the entire Bible. The word "rest" is the Greek word *sabbatismos*, a direct reference to the Sabbath day of the week of millennia (see chapter 3, "The Outline of the Ages").

Strong's #4520 has a definition for *sabbatismos* that is remarkably accurate. It says that this is "the blessed rest from the toils and troubles looked for in the age to come by the true worshippers of God and true Christians."

Andrew Murray said in *The Holiest of All*:[1]

> There remaineth therefore a Sabbath rest for the people of God: taken in connection with what precedes about the seventh day or Sabbath, the rest is here called a *sabbatism* or a sabbath rest. It is spoken of as remaining, with reference to the rest in Caanan. That was but a shadow and symbol: the real Sabbath rest remained, waiting its time, till Christ the true Joshua should come, and open it to us by Himself entering it.

Another major reference to the millennial kingdom, and the judgment to be made for those entering into it, is contained in verse 12.

> *For the word of God is quick, and powerful, and sharper than any twoedged sword,*

> *piercing even to the dividing asunder of soul and spirit, and of the joints and marrow, and is a discerner of the thoughts and intents of the heart.*   *Hebrews 4:12*

Although this verse is often used to verify the depth and power of the written Scriptures, and without argument it can be, the more specific reference is to Jesus' judgment. He is the Word of God—the Incarnate Word of God. We know that this is referring to Him, because the next verse says that all things are open to His sight.

> *Neither is there any creature that is not manifest in his sight: but all things are naked and opened unto the eyes of him with whom we have to do.*   *Hebrews 4:13*

This is important because it says that the Incarnate Word divides soul and spirit, which are judged at different times and by different standards. The spirit of a Christian has already been saved and therefore has been judged as holy and righteous. The soul, on the other hand, is what will be judged at the judgment seat of Christ. Jesus can, and will, divide the soul from the spirit along with the intentions of the heart and not just the actions of an individual. All of this judgment determines either entry into the kingdom of heaven and the *sabbatismos* rest, or the casting out into outer darkness.

We have learned some interesting things from this chapter dealing with comparisons between the children of Israel and the church. The greatest truth we have learned is that we must labor while we are still alive to enter into the rest of the millennial kingdom. Certainly, all Christians have ceased from laboring in order to be justified before God by their works, but we should all be about the Father's business and laboring to build His kingdom on earth now.

While it's true that we have to labor, we also need to be good and faithful, press toward the mark of the high calling, and have works that will pass the test of fire, in order to enter into the coming 1,000-year kingdom. All of these criteria, plus more from the gospel of Matthew, will show us the keys to entering the kingdom.

CHAPTER 13
KEYS TO ENTERING THE KINGDOM

After laying the background that we have, this chapter becomes the most important aspect of our entire study. There are two gospels—of grace and of the kingdom—and there are two inheritances—grace and rewards. To enter the kingdom of the Father, we simply had to believe on Jesus and receive the gift of eternal life and, with it, we obtained the right to enter His eternal kingdom. But working faithfully in the family business now and showing ourselves worthy to rule and reign with the Lord is what will qualify us for the kingdom of the Son. There are keys to entering this kingdom, and it is of paramount importance that we see and understand them. I discovered these keys in two ways. One was a simple matter of asking my computer to read the Bible and find all the verses where the words "enter" and "kingdom" were used in the same verse. The other way was much more exacting. I had to read the Bible and search for the places where the kingdom was referenced in the scope of the text and then decipher the requirements from each context. My findings are quite comprehensive, and even though there are numerous details involved, I want to point out the greatest of all the keys—that is, to follow the Holy Spirit.

The reason the Lord sent the Holy Spirit is because we need Him. His job is to help us qualify for Jesus' kingdom and He will do this by leading us. His job is to lead; ours is to follow.

The simplest way to instruct someone to enter the 1,000-year reign is to teach them to be led by the Holy Spirit. People have a common misconception that to be led by the Holy Spirit only involves walking in the empowering of the gifts of the Spirit. This is only a part of the requirements. Just as Rebekah was a working bride, as seen by her watering the camels, so we need to work in service through the gifts of the Holy Spirit. This is not the entirety of the matter, however; we also need to follow the Holy Spirit as He leads us in holiness. We also need to follow His leading in perseverance, attitude, obedience, and faithfulness.

We will find that the Word of God agrees with the Holy Spirit in the keys for entering the kingdom. This is only logical, since the Word of God came from holy men who were moved (led) by the Holy Spirit (2 Peter 1:21).

Concerning being led by the Holy Spirit and entering the millennial kingdom, I recently had an altercation with a brother in the Lord that bears mentioning. He is a very fine man, had accompanied me on several mission trips, and really loves the Lord. Unfortunately, he has fallen into a cult that teaches that Christians must keep certain laws to be righteous before the Lord. When I read Romans 8:4 to him, it really gave him problems, as well it should, because that verse firmly states that the righteousness of the law comes by walking after, or by, the Holy Spirit. I continue to pray for him and all those who think that they can lift themselves up by their own bootstraps.

Yes, there are requirements to enter the millennial kingdom, but if righteousness came by the works of the law, then Christ died in vain (Galatians 2:21). We will go through many verses and requirements in our study about entering the kingdom, but remember that the greatest of these will be to follow the Holy Spirit. Matthew 7:21–23 says that even if you do good works but do not know the Lord personally and intimately, you too will be cast into the outer darkness.

So, please do not let the keys we are going to discuss become a list of rules and regulations, because they are not meant to replace intimacy with the Lord. The Lord choosing someone who is burdened by rules and regulations for His kingdom would be like a man choosing a bride solely because she was meticulous and had worked hard to put on make-up and dress up for him. That may be part of the selection process, but more importantly, he should consider the character of the woman and how much she loves him.

Matthew Chapters 5–7

Matthew chapters 5–7 contain teachings about entering into the millennial kingdom with the Lord. This section commences with Jesus leaving a multitude at the bottom of a mountain and the disciples following him to the top in 5:1 and ends with Him coming back down the mountain in 8:1. The beginning discourse is called the Beatitudes. "Beatitude" means "beautiful saying," but these sayings of Jesus are not always beautiful sayings—they are often hard words. When people read or sing these words, they are reciting the requirements to reign with Jesus on the earth.

Jesus opened His mouth and began by saying, "Blessed are the poor in spirit: for theirs is the kingdom of heaven." The phrase, "kingdom of heaven" is used five times in this section of Scripture, and all allude to that present time and also to the future reign of Jesus on the earth. Within this section of Scripture are commandments that demand discipleship and not just believing. All of the Beatitudes contain requirements, such as: be meek, be merciful, be peacemakers, and be pure in heart, because you will be persecuted. This is disciple talk.

There are other demands made upon disciples within this section of Scripture, and all of these relate to entering the kingdom of heaven.

> *For I say unto you, That except your righteousness shall exceed the righteousness of the scribes and Pharisees, ye shall in no case enter into the kingdom of heaven.*
> *Matthew 5:20*

Within this section is the Lord's Prayer, too. Every Sunday, or whenever many Christians meet, they pray this prayer. I wonder if they really mean it, because if they did, the whole character of Christianity would change. What would happen if people really sought the will of God on earth and forgave others so that they could be forgiven? It does say, "for thine is the kingdom."

Other requirements are: take no thought for tomorrow; lay up for yourself treasures in heaven; judge not; seek ye first the kingdom of God; and enter in by the strait gate. Finally Matthew 7:21–23 tells us that just our works without true intimacy will not get us into this kingdom.

There are other places in the Word of God that provide requirements for the 1,000-year reign, but none other is as specific and direct as Matthew chapters 5–7.

Repent

We covered earlier that the requirement to receive the gospel of grace and the inheritance of eternal life in the new heavens and earth was to believe. Now we will see specifically that the requirement to enter the millennial reign is to repent. John the Baptist preached it.

> *And saying, Repent ye: for the kingdom of heaven is at hand.*
> *Matthew 3:2*

Jesus preached it, too.

> *From that time Jesus began to preach, and to say, Repent: for the kingdom of heaven is at hand.*   *Matthew 4:17*

"To repent" means to change the way you are living, and its true essence includes following the ways of the Lord. This is a requirement for the 1,000-year reign. The Holy Spirit was sent to convict you (John 16:7–8), so listen to Him if you want to be found worthy to reign with Jesus.

Take Care of Your Physical Body

First Corinthians 9:27 has a message to all disciples.

> *But I keep under my body, and bring it into subjection: lest that by any means, when I have preached to others, I myself should be a castaway.*   *1 Corinthians 9:27*

"Keeping under your body" literally means to "beat it down black and blue," not letting it dominate you. You must bring it into subjection. Otherwise, when you preach to others, you would still be a castaway. The usage of "castaway" is indicative of an understanding of the millennial kingdom. The New International Version translates this verse well.

> *No, I beat my body and make it my slave so that after I have preached to others, I myself will not be disqualified for the prize.*
>   *1 Corinthians 9:27 NIV*

The prize mentioned here is the 1,000-year reign on the earth with Jesus. The context can be found by starting in verse 17.

> *For if I do this thing willingly, I have a reward: but if against my will, a dispensation*

of the gospel is committed unto me.
1 Corinthians 9:17

This deals with a dispensation of the gospel—the millennial kingdom reign. It is a whole time period and administration given to those who strive for the mastery, compete for the prize and learn to fight not as one who beats the air. Those who do these things will receive a crown that does not corrupt (verse 25).

The Bible tells us that he who is faithful in least will also be faithful in much (Luke 16:10), and that among the spirit, soul, and body, the least is your body. Likewise, exhortation is given that if you properly steward the possessions on earth, then the true riches of the kingdom will be given to you, also.

We have already seen from Philippians 3:21 that those individuals who suffer for the Lord will be the ones receiving their glorified bodies; now 1 Corinthians 9:27 directly tells us that if we preach good things, but neglect to care for our bodies, then we could be disqualified from the prize of the millennial reign.

All of us have bodies of corrupting flesh. That is an undeniable fact, but how we steward them is of grave consequence, especially if we do not do it properly. Yes, it may just be flesh, but if your earthly house falls apart, you will have no place to live to finish out your destiny.

In a class I was teaching once, there was a beautiful lady graced with a powerful anointing. I reached out to her and availed to help her sing and minister in different places. I even wanted to take her to India on a missions trip. She declined. When I asked her why, she said, "I don't want to disgrace God, because I smoke." This caused some deep understanding to grow and come out of me.

Let us say that God has destined you to live to be 80 years old and the last 15 years of your life were to be the most fruitful and profitable for Him. However, because of poor habits (like overeating, lack of exercise, smoking, or drinking) your body corrupted early and you died at 65. When you appear before the Lord at the judgment seat of Christ, He says, "The last 15 pages of your account ledger are blank." You respond, "I don't understand. I faithfully served until the day I died." He then says, "Yes, you did; but you died early because you did not keep under your body. Furthermore," He might say, "During the last 15 years of your life I had you scheduled to bring over a thousand people into the family, but because of your lack of discipline, they never heard. Depart into outer darkness you wicked and slothful servant."

Maybe this causes fear to come upon you. Good—fear is a strong motivator. Jesus used it a lot when he said, "Depart into the outer darkness where there will be weeping and gnashing of teeth."

Keep under your body and bring it into subjection, so that you will be qualified for the kingdom.

Strive for the Masteries

To be crowned in the millennial kingdom, you must contend earnestly for the faith; you must strive for the masteries.

> *And if a man also strive for masteries, yet is he not crowned, except he strive lawfully.*
> *2 Timothy 2:5*

If you are going to run in a track meet, you must stay in your lane. Or, if you take a short cut in a cross-country meet, you will be disqualified and will not receive the prize. You must strive lawfully and you must strive for the masteries. The phrase "strive for the masteries" is the Greek word *athleo*, obviously from which we get the word "athletics."

We already dealt with this truth in 1 Corinthians 9:25, where it states that you must strive for the mastery. Those words come from the Greek word *agonizomai*. We get our word "agony" from this source.

Athletes agonize over their training and conditioning. If you want to be crowned, you must agonize to win. Vince Lombardi, the legendary football coach of the Green Bay Packers, once said, "Winning isn't everything—it is the *only* thing." You must have this attitude.

Attitude will determine actions—how often you take them and how fervently you perform them. The attitude of striving for the masteries will determine not just that you serve but how zealously you do it.

To enter the kingdom, you must strive for the masteries.

Give Diligence to Make Your Calling and Election Sure

Second Peter 1:4–11 provides a magnificent truth concerning entering the kingdom. Verse 10 is the one that tells us to be diligent to make our calling and election sure.

> *Wherefore the rather, brethren, give diligence to make your calling and election sure: for if ye do these things, ye shall never fall.*
> 2 *Peter 1:10*

Verse 11 tells us why we should.

> *For so an entrance shall be ministered unto you abundantly into the everlasting kingdom of our Lord and Saviour Jesus Christ.*
> 2 *Peter 1:11*

This verse states as clearly as any other place in the Bible that the kingdom of Jesus Christ is to be earned, not just given by grace. The context of this verse goes back to verse 4 and grants tremendous insight into some deep understanding.

Second Peter 1:4 says that we might become partakers of the divine nature by the promises of the Word of God. It further goes on to say in the following verses that we must give all diligence to add certain things to the divinely given nature we received by grace. Notice the admonition of diligence given in verses 5 and 10. If we diligently add these things to our graciously given divine nature, we will become partakers of it. Partaker means a "full sharer," coming from the Greek word *koinonos*, a sharer and a partner.

If we give diligence to add faith, knowledge, temperance, patience, godliness, brotherly kindness, and charity to our gift of grace, we will be sure not to fall or come short of the kingdom, and we will become a partner, or a joint-heir, with Jesus in the millennial kingdom.

Once again, we find that we must add something to the grace already given to us in order to enter Jesus' kingdom. God moved in Christ Jesus; now it is our move. We must give diligence and virtuously add works to our blessings if we are to gain an entrance into the kingdom of our Lord Jesus Christ.

Finish the Fight

We studied earlier that the Apostle Paul said in Philippians 3:11 NKJ, "if by any means, I may attain to the resurrection [*exanastasis*—the out resurrection] from the dead." This was written early in Paul's ministry, and even though he had already accomplished great things for the kingdom of God upon the earth, he had not yet lived his full life span and completed the task given him. We will see now that toward the end of his life Paul knew he had attained the out resurrection and, in fact, knew that he would receive a crown for his rewards and reign with the Lord in the coming kingdom.

> *For I am now ready to be offered, and the time of my departure is at hand. I have fought a good fight, I have finished my course, I have kept the faith: Henceforth there is laid up for me a crown of righteousness, which the Lord, the righteous judge, shall give me at that day: and not to me only, but unto all them also that love his appearing.* 2 Timothy 4:6–8

Paul had completed his course and finished his fight. There are requirements to enter into the kingdom of our Lord and receive the crowns that are available to those who will sit upon thrones with the Lord (Revelation 20:4). The Lord had revealed to Paul that his work was almost done and that he would receive his rewards and be in the millennial kingdom with Him.

This requirement of standing all the days of your life and fulfilling your destiny is recorded in Revelation 2:10.

> *Be thou faithful unto death, and I will give thee a crown of life.* Revelation 2:10b

Being faithful means being faithful all the way to the very end. Oh, what a day that will be, when we see Jesus and receive the rewards that He has to give us! What great days and length of life we will enjoy as we enter into the joy of the Lord and the kingdom that has been prepared since before the foundation of the world! Galatians 6:9 again testifies of this truth.

> *And let us not be weary in well doing: for in due season we shall reap, if we faint not.*
> Galatians 6:9

In summary of this chapter and section, we have learned that in order to enter the kingdom of our Lord and His 1,000-year reign, we must earn it.

At the judgment seat of Christ, we will learn if we

- have warranted a worthy judgment;
- have a seat reserved at the marriage supper of the Lamb;
- have earned the right to ride on a white horse to return to the earth with the Lord to reign with Him.

We have seen the requirements of

- being a working bride;
- being a good and faithful servant;
- laboring while it is still this day, so that we can rest in the day (of the Lord) yet to come.

Finally, we have seen some keys to entering the kingdom of the Lord. Remember that the Lord sent the Holy Spirit to help us prepare for the judgment seat of Christ. What we have covered is by no means the extent of what the Lord requires, but enough of the whole subject to understand that the Lord wants you to work to earn the reward of inheritance. The table on the following page will help to summarize the keys to entering the kingdom and provide scripture references for documentation.

Keys to Entering the Kingdom

Be led by the Holy Spirit	Romans 8:14
Make your calling and election sure	2 Peter 1:10–11
Your righteousness must exceed that of the Pharisees	Matthew 5:20
Seek the Lord, not power	Matthew 7:21–22
Seek the kingdom, not riches	Matthew 19:23–24
Become as a little child	Matthew 18:3
Be born again	John 3:5–6
Endure suffering through tribulation	Acts 14:22
Work (the proper wedding garment)	Matthew 22:12
Have faith	Matthew 8:12
Be good and faithful	Matthew 25:30

Please keep in mind, especially as we move into the subject of the next section, "Missing the Kingdom," that according to Luke 12:32, it is the Father's good pleasure to give us the kingdom. Let us not be weary in well doing. In due season we *shall* reap, if we faint not.

SECTION FOUR
MISSING THE KINGDOM

As a personal preference, I would prefer to leave this section out and, in all honesty, I hope that my research of the Scriptures has been wrong. I do not want to see anyone miss the glory of the millennial kingdom. But the Lord did not put me in charge, nor am I on the steering committee for end-time decisions. If what we are about to study is true, and of course I surely believe that it is, the vast, vast majority of Christians are going to be greatly surprised when they meet Jesus.

It is a good thing to realize that you do not have to know about the 1,000-year reign to enter into it. However, it will be very beneficial to know in order to prepare for it, and to follow the Holy Spirit as He works to get you in. I think of my grandmother who labored in prayer for me and all her children and grandchildren, and died, not knowing about the rewards that would be hers for her faithful service. Although it is not my decision as to who will enter the kingdom, I can't imagine that she could possibly miss it.

Missing the kingdom will be a harsh reality for some people. If they have thought that they could get saved and live like the devil or even in a lazy state, they will find that the Lord is totally fair. He will reward those who have worked and not reward those who have not. In addition, He will punish those, even His own children, who have worked against the purposes of His kingdom.

Could there be anything worse than missing the kingdom? In chapter 14, "Seeing the Kingdom, but Not Entering," we will find that there will be those who see the kingdom from a distance, but will know that their sins have excluded them from entering. Remember the parable of the good and faithful servant versus the wicked and slothful? Chapter 15, "The Outer Darkness," will serve as a wake-up call for those who have been slothful. Chapter 16, "Gehenna," will be a warning to those who have been wicked. Chapter 17, "The Close of the Kingdom," will give comfort to those who do miss Jesus' kingdom, as they realize that the time spent being away from the Lord's presence (or even in the punishment of Gehenna) will have an end, and they will enter into the kingdom of the Father by their inheritance of grace.

CHAPTER 14
SEEING THE KINGDOM BUT NOT ENTERING IT

In the life of Moses we find a profile of seeing the kingdom but not being able to enter it. This relates to the outer darkness, a place where the inhabitants will be able to see the millennial kingdom but will not be able to enter it. We learn of this in John 3:3 and 5.

> *Jesus answered and said unto him, Verily, verily, I say unto thee, Except a man be born again, he cannot see the kingdom of God.*
> *John 3:3*

> *Jesus answered, Verily, verily, I say unto thee, Except a man be born of water and of the Spirit, he cannot enter into the kingdom of God.*
> *John 3:5*

The beginning of this profile originates when Moses sins by striking the rock at Meribah to make water come out of it. Exodus 17:6 is the account where Moses struck the rock and water came out the first time. But in Numbers 20:8, Moses was to speak to the rock in order for the water to come out. Instead, because of his anger (sin), he struck the rock to make the water come out. Because of this sin, Moses was not allowed to go into the Promised Land.

(Many have questioned why God punished Moses so severely for this. My speculation is that this episode was meant to portray our entrée to Jesus [the Rock]. To gain access to Him, He first had to be beaten, but now all we have to do is [speak] ask Him and He comes to us.)

Regardless of why God's judgment was so severe, Moses was forbidden to enter into the Promised Land (which is a type for the 1,000-year kingdom).

> *And the LORD spake unto Moses and Aaron, Because ye believed me not, to sanctify me in the eyes of the children of Israel, therefore ye shall not bring this congregation into the land which I have given them.   Numbers 20:12*

Although Moses was not allowed to enter the Promised Land, he was allowed to see it from Mount Nebo.

> *Because ye trespassed against me among the children of Israel at the waters of Meribah Kadesh, in the wilderness of Zin; because ye sanctified me not in the midst of the children of Israel. Yet thou shalt see the land before thee; but thou shalt not go thither unto the land which I give the children of Israel.*
> *Deuteronomy 32:51–52*

This is relative to the outer darkness. Jesus will say to those who have sinned despite their access to Him, "Depart into the outer darkness." In other words, they will be able to see the kingdom but not enter it, just as Moses was able to see the Promised Land but not enter it. John 3:3 and 5 reveal the criteria to see and enter the millennial kingdom.

John 3:3 says that it is available to see the kingdom just by being born again; John 3:5 says to enter it, you must be born of water and of the spirit. On the surface, it appears that these are the same, but there is a deeper truth to be found.

To "be born again," the phrase used in John 3:3, is the total aspect of God's gracious gift to you. But to "be born of water and of the Spirit," (John 3:5) although it communicates a similar concept, requires that you separate the flesh (water) from the Spirit (that which has been born again).

The hidden truth conveyed in these verses is that if you want to *see* the kingdom, you must be born again, but if you want to *enter* the kingdom, you must discern the difference between flesh and Spirit and strive to walk by the Spirit and not by the flesh (Romans 8:8).

Moses saw the Promised Land but never went into it because of sin. As Christian believers, we will all see the millennial kingdom because of God's grace, but if we want to enter it, we must walk after the things of the Spirit or we will be looking at it from the outer darkness.

CHAPTER 15
THE OUTER DARKNESS

Sometimes I peruse the table of contents in a book and skip ahead to read a particular section. If you have done this, it is your prerogative, but you may have exposed yourself to a measurable amount of fear without having read the previous sections in preparation. I have purposely waited to put this chapter toward the end to build a foundation of understanding for this topic.

I originally taught this material in a class called The Gospel of the Kingdom and released it in a set of audiocassette tapes.[1] However, I have waited until the forming of this book to write this chapter so that it can be set within the proper framework of an understanding of the gospel of grace and the two inheritances.

Before venturing into this study, please remember that the inheritance of grace has been given to all Christians and, because it is a gift of grace, you will never lose it. If just getting saved satisfies you, then I may think you are foolish or more probably ignorant; but if that's all you want, then that is all you will get. But for those individuals who serve the Lord with their whole heart and want to be with Him always, God will reward them for their faithfulness.

The Outer Darkness

To provide an outline of this chapter, I will set forth the scriptural evidence of the outer darkness. In addition to explaining the word usages of "outer" and "darkness," I will go through the who, what, where, when, why, and how of it. This is an intriguing and complex study, so please excuse the lengthiness of this for the sake of being thorough. This is by no means the last word on this subject, but I hope that it will be among the first of many.

Because of scriptural evidence, I firmly believe that the outer darkness is an actual place. If you embrace this as truth after searching out the matter in its entirety, the fear of the Lord will increase dramatically in your life. The outer darkness will exist in heaven while the millennial kingdom transpires on earth. Those individuals whose works do not merit entering into the 1,000-year reign of Jesus on the earth will wait in the outer darkness, weeping and gnashing their teeth while they are there, knowing that they could have been enjoying Jesus' kingdom on the earth if they had been good and faithful.

Scriptural Evidence for the Outer Darkness

Even though there are only three actual usages of this phrase, all of them are written in red ink in my Bible, because they are the words of Jesus.

> *But the children of the kingdom shall be cast out into outer darkness: there shall be weeping and gnashing of teeth.*   Matthew 8:12

All of these come from the gospel of Matthew, and that is understandable, since Matthew portrays Jesus as the King, and the outer darkness will be comprised of His unfaithful subjects.

These usages all have a common truth interwoven into the verses; each of them describes the activity going on there—weeping and gnashing of teeth. Weeping will be done by those who are sad; gnashing the teeth will be done by those who are mad.

Weeping and gnashing of teeth reminds me of when I tried out for the basketball team in high school. To make it, you could not be cut, or in other words, you had to qualify for the team. I remember reading my name on the list and the jubilation that came upon me. In the midst of my jumping around and whooping and yelling, I distinctly remember two other boys reading the list at the same time. When their names were not on it, one began crying and the other began yelling in anger. One said, "I could have made it if I had just worked harder." The other began cursing and said, "I'm better than that guy. This is BS and all politics." He smashed his hand on the locker as he stormed out of the room. These are the reactions of those who will not "make the cut."

There are two other usages of outer darkness in Matthew 22:13 and 25:30, and we will examine them momentarily, but the textual usages of "weeping and gnashing of teeth" open other scriptures that provide insight into the outer darkness.

> *And shall cut him asunder, and appoint him his portion with the hypocrites: there shall be weeping and gnashing of teeth.*
> *Matthew 24:51*

> *There shall be weeping and gnashing of teeth, when ye shall see Abraham, and Isaac, and Jacob, and all the prophets, in the kingdom of God, and you yourselves thrust out.*
> *Luke 13:28*

Matthew 24:51 reveals the judgment of the outer darkness and weeping and gnashing of teeth for those who abuse their leadership position and take advantage of those the Lord gave them to steward. Luke 13:28 deals with those that the Lord does not know. This also cross references Matthew 7:21–23, where the Lord commands those to depart from Him who had done miracles, spoken prophecies, and cast out demons, because He did not know them.

The Outer Darkness

Matthew 22:13 gives more textual evidence about this place of separation. This verse deals with the one who is at the marriage supper and does not have on the proper attire. (See chapter 7, "The Bride Comes Out of the Body.") This amply demonstrates that we must work to enter the kingdom and also be on intimate terms with the Lord, as a bride is with her bridegroom.

> *Then said the king to the servants, Bind him hand and foot, and take him away, and cast him into outer darkness, there shall be weeping and gnashing of teeth.*
> *Matthew 22:13*

Matthew 25:30 has the next usage of the phrase and this verse deals with the unfaithful servant. He was punished because he was wicked and slothful.

> *And cast ye the unprofitable servant into outer darkness: there shall be weeping and gnashing of teeth.   Matthew 25:30*

All of these scriptures reinforce the absolute truth that there *is* such a place. I believe I already shared the cartoon about the three guys descending into hell on the escalator with one of them saying to the other two, "You don't have to worry. Our elders voted 3 out of 5 that this place does not exist." The point here is the same—you don't have to believe in this place to go there. Likewise, you don't have to know about the millennial reign to go there either, but it does increase our chances if we know where we are going and why we will go there.

The following table will summarize the usages of scripture mentioning the outer darkness and weeping and gnashing of teeth and why those individuals were sent there.

Word Usages of "Outer" and "Darkness"

Reference	Usage	Criterion for Judgment
Matthew 8:12	Outer darkness / Weeping and gnashing of teeth	Children of the kingdom not having faith
Matthew 22:13	Outer darkness / Weeping and gnashing of teeth	Not having proper attire (works) at the marriage of the Son
Matthew 24:51	Weeping and gnashing of teeth	Abuse of goods and people and not looking for the Lord
Matthew 25:30	Outer darkness / Weeping and gnashing of teeth	Being wicked and/or slothful
Luke 13:28	Weeping and gnashing of teeth	Not knowing the Lord, even though working for Him

The Greek words for both "outer" and "darkness" give the indication that this description is an actual place. A fellow workman of the Word of God once asked me, "Does it bother you that there is no article 'the' accompanying the Greek

The Outer Darkness

words 'outer darkness'?" "No," I said, "since there is no article 'the' in the Aramaic text in which Matthew was originally written." Upon closer scrutiny of the three usages of outer darkness in Matthew in the Greek, however, not only is the article "the" present, but it is used with both the word "outer" and the word "darkness." Look at the Greek rendering of this. The bold and underlined words are the definite article "the."

> οι δε υιοι της βασιλειας εκβληθησονται εις **το** σκοτος **το** εξωτερον εκει εσται ο κλαυθμος και ο βρυγμος των οδοντων   Matthew 8:12

The usage of the article "the" in the critical Greek text shows that at least the translator of Matthew believed that there is, or will be, such a place. He even emphasized it by saying "the outer the darkness." This is the usage in every occurrence of the words. With the use of a double article "the," the proper translation into the English would have been "the Outer Darkness," since this typically indicates a proper noun (one naming a particular person, place, or thing) in the Greek. I have refrained from this usage until now, but believe that textual evidence should give me the right to capitalize it.

More insight can be gained about the Outer Darkness from the words "outer" and "darkness." "Outer" is *exoteros*, from which we get the words "exit" and "exoteric." "Exoteric" literally means "outside." Tracing its etymology, the origin is *exo* which means "without" or "outdoors." The deeper root, *ek*, means "coming out of." So, we can deduce that "outer" means "outside" or "outside the door," or something that has been removed to the outside.

Since the usage of "cast" is in all the verses (Matthew 8:12, 22:13, and 25:30) we can very clearly deduce that whoever is cast into the Outer Darkness is cast out of some other place. (The word for "cast" is the same word used when referring to "casting out a demon.") So, whoever is cast into the Outer

Darkness, is cast out of wherever the light is. We see this verified by studying the word "darkness."

"Darkness" is the Greek word *skotos*. It is used 31 times in the New Testament and is translated "darkness" in every usage. The simplest definition of darkness is "absence of light." So, wherever the Outer Darkness is, it is outside of the light. In other words, to use the teaching of Matthew 22:13 and 14, many are called into the light, but few will remain in it.

Where is the Outer Darkness?

Thus far, we have covered what the Outer Darkness is and who will go there. We will now discuss where this place of Outer Darkness is. There is some speculation over this issue, and to be quite honest, I have found very few resources to consult, since there are almost no listings of "the Outer Darkness" in concordances or Bible dictionaries.

There is only a limited number of possibilities for where the Outer Darkness could be. Revelation 5:13 lists all the viable possibilities—in heaven, on earth, under the earth, or in the sea. Determining its location is a biblical interpretive exercise, since there is no verse that says "the Outer Darkness is located at _____."

The most likely geographical candidate is heaven. The truth that we will have to pass through the judgment seat of Christ, which is in the heavens, makes it seem logical that the Outer Darkness would be there as well. My particular belief is that it does not yet exist, but that it will, at a future time, be located in heaven. When we look at a comparison of those suffering there for the duration of time that they do, versus those participating in the millennial kingdom, it seems even more plausible that it will be in the heavens—especially since the millennial kingdom and its inhabitants will be on the earth. We will see in chapter 17, "The Close of the Kingdom," that the Lord Jesus will gather all things together both in heaven and on earth, and will present them to God the Father for the commencement of the kingdom of the Father in the new heavens and earth (Ephesians 1:10). Based upon this scriptural evidence, my personal belief is that the Outer Darkness will exist in the heavens after the judgment seat of Christ.

When Will the Outer Darkness Exist?

Bible texts concur that when someone dies now, they either go to hell or paradise. Hell is for the unrighteous dead, and paradise is for the righteous dead. Therefore, some preliminary distinction must be made concerning a person at the time of their departure from their physical body. However, as we have seen, there is a time of judgment coming at the judgment seat of Christ, and its timing will also determine the timing of the Outer Darkness.

Second Timothy 4:1 tells us that Jesus will judge upon His appearing and at His kingdom. This is important because the Outer Darkness will not be used until the Lord has judged a person worthy or unworthy to enter His kingdom. In my opinion, which I believe is scripturally based, the judgment seat of Christ does not occur until all those people who will believe upon Jesus are saved. That would be well into the great tribulation when numerous martyrs will sacrifice their lives during the harvest at the end of the age.

In other words, the Outer Darkness does not exist until people are judged, and I do not believe that happens until Jesus judges them at His appearing and in His kingdom. It is interesting to note that if someone would affix the judgment seat of Christ at the time of an individual's death, then the Outer Darkness could possibly exist now. This would be very similar to the Roman Catholic concept of purgatory. (Let me clearly state that I do not believe the idea of purgatory is based on Scripture, and that there certainly is no biblical provision for praying or paying anyone out of something they have worked their way into.)

I am diligent to say "I believe" this or that on these issues, because I cannot make absolute statements about these matters. In summary, concerning the timing of the Outer Darkness, I believe that Christians go to paradise when they die and wait till all the dead in Christ have died before the judgment seat of Christ begins. After that, they will either go to the marriage supper of the Lamb and then on to the millennial kingdom, or to the Outer Darkness, or to Gehenna (as discussed in the next chapter).

Why is There an Outer Darkness?

Obviously the only one qualified to answer this question is the Lord. However, God is no respecter of persons. He loves all His children and rewards each for simply being His child and also for faithfully serving Him. The Outer Darkness is a period of "time out" for disobedient children. It will not actually qualify as punishment, but a period of time when the children will reflect and realize how foolish they have been.

When we get to the topic of Gehenna, we will cover the punishment aspect of God's retribution toward His people. Certain of His children have not only been lazy, but they have also done bad or wicked things. Even though God dearly loves all of His children, He will not allow all of those things to go unpunished.

So, why is there an Outer Darkness? God will give a time out for lazy children to think about what they should have done—that is the purpose for the Outer Darkness. He will also administer punishment for those children who have done wickedly—that is the purpose for Gehenna.

In closing this chapter, I would like to make a comment about 1 Thessalonians 4:17, since certain questions usually arise concerning the Outer Darkness. It says that those who are gathered together to the Lord will ever be with the Lord. This verse bothered me for quite some time until I realized that the word "with" is the Greek word *sun*. *Sun* means "in association with." There is another Greek preposition, *meta*, that means "in company with."

Those individuals who will be in the Outer Darkness will be in association with the Lord, much the same as we are now present in the body and absent from the Lord. The Lord will not forsake them and leave them in the Outer Darkness for all eternity, but will someday gather together all things in heaven and in earth and deliver everything up to the Father. They may be physically absent from Him, but they will be with Him in association, the Lord knowing that He will return and bring them unto Himself.

How Long Will the Outer Darkness Last?

Earlier in chapter 3, "The Outline of the Ages," we covered the verses from 2 Peter 3:8 and Psalm 90:4 that reveal and stipulate one day with the Lord is as a thousand years. This has great bearing on how long the Outer Darkness (and Gehenna) will last.

Philippians 3:21 tells us that those who faithfully serve the Lord will receive a glorious body fashioned like unto the Lord's. This means that one of the major rewards of service and blessing in the millennial reign will be to have a body. That would be a good idea, since that is what those individuals will live in while on earth. (We are spirit beings in earth suits.)

This is relative to the discussion of the length of the Outer Darkness, because those within a body will realize and experience the millennial kingdom for 1,000 years, but those outside of a body, those who did not earn the reward of a glorified body, will suffer for one day (in the Lord's manner of reckoning).

The 1,000 Year Reign of Jesus Christ on the Earth

> *But, beloved, be not ignorant of this one thing, that one day is with the Lord as a thousand years, and a thousand years as one day.*
>
> *2 Peter 3:8*

When a spirit being enters a physical body, time decelerates. At the judgment seat of Christ, when a person passes the test of fire, he will receive a body that cannot be burned. That individual will at some point re-enter a physical body to descend with the Lord to reign on the earth. Many times, I hear people talking about being perpetually 30 years young. That will be true for those who merit a new body by faithful service. The reign of the Lord will last 1,000 years or about 12,000 months or 365,000 days. This will be virtually ageless living.

Those individuals called but not chosen will not receive a new body. Consequently, time will not decelerate for them but will continue at the rate it has since they left their physical body on earth. So how long will the Outer Darkness last for them? One day! But that will be their longest day, because they will be fully conscious of the 1,000 years of bliss they could have enjoyed if they had been faithful.

> *O the depth of the riches both of the wisdom and knowledge of God! how unsearchable are his judgments, and his ways past finding out!*
>
> *Romans 11:33*

God maximizes the blessings and minimizes the pain. Our God is an awesome God!

So, the Outer Darkness is a time out for lazy children, but we will find in the next chapter that Gehenna is punishment for rebellious children. God loves them all, but whom He loves He chastens (Hebrews 12:6; Revelation 3:19).

CHAPTER 16
GEHENNA

In the previous chapter, I compared two places where people who fail the judgment seat of Christ will go. They will go to either a time out or a punishment. The Outer Darkness is the comparison to time out, where there appears to be no punishment inflicted but rather sitting and watching the "other kids play," causing those in the Outer Darkness to either weep or gnash their teeth. Gehenna is the place of punishment for rebellion and disobedience; it is the place that God has reserved for those individuals who wreak havoc within the church and destroy what they were sent to build.

Before presenting my research on Gehenna, I need to be clear about this subject. There are more resources of study about Gehenna (*ge'enna*) than there are for the Outer Darkness. Unfortunately, most of these materials simply equate Gehenna to hell. This unfounded comparison deserves our special attention and further clarification.

Gehenna is equated to hell by certain Bible students due to improper translation and its correlation to "fire." Both of these places exist and both involve punishment by fire. This would be like saying Wrigley Field and Yankee Stadium are the same place, since baseball is played in each location. Actually Gehenna is related to fire more so in the Bible than hell. Hell's relation to fire involves the lake of fire, but Gehenna is descriptively called "hell fire" several times (Matthew 5:22, 18:9; Mark 9:47; and James 3:6).

My belief is that hell is a different place than Gehenna, because of those who will be sent there. Hell (from the Greek word *hades* and the Hebrew word *sheowl*) is the underworld and the destiny of all disobedient spirits, particularly the unsaved. It is also translated generically as "the grave." Psalm 9:17 says "the wicked shall be turned into hell, and all the nations that forget God." Revelation 20:13 and 14 also say that death and hell will give up their dead and will be cast into the lake of fire.

Gehenna, unlike hell, is a place for the righteous dead who need to be punished or purified. Jesus threatened His own apostles with being sent there (Mark 9:43, 45, and 47). We will see an abundance of related documentation throughout this chapter and other reasons why Gehenna is not *hades* or *sheowl*.

The actual word *gehenna* comes from an Old Testament usage of the Valley of Hinnom (i.e., Joshua 15:8; 2 Kings 23:10). Its relation to fire is that it was here that the children of Israel made their children "pass through the fire" in dedication to Molech, and because of this, God designated it as the burning trash dump for Jerusalem (Jeremiah 7:31–33). This is very important to keep in mind, because these fires will eventually be extinguished during the millennial kingdom.

So as you study this, please bear in mind that the words "hell" and "Gehenna" involve different words and different locations. Not remembering this could cause you undue confusion. Regardless of what you call it, God has a place of punishment reserved for His servants who are rebellious, disobedient, and abusive toward the people He gave them to oversee. This is a much more severe place of sentencing than the Outer Darkness.

Gehenna is for Leaders and Apostate Ministers

God is no respecter of persons, but to whom much is given, much will be required. As we study Gehenna, we will see that God does not pull any punches with His leaders. He placed leaders in charge of His people and if they abuse them and take advantage of them, He will justly punish those leaders by sentencing them to Gehenna.

Jesus' teaching about Gehenna is very clear. He told His apostles and leaders that if they caused "the little ones" to fall and be offended, then they would be punished. He warned them of this three times in Mark chapter 9.

> *And if thy hand offend thee, cut it off: it is better for thee to enter into life maimed, than having two hands to go into hell [Gehenna], into the fire that never shall be quenched.*
> *Mark 9:43*

This lesson should speak loudly to leaders within the body of Christ. Jesus told the 12 apostles that if they viewed their hands (verse 43—their works), their feet (verse 45—the way they walked), or their eyes (verse 47—the way they looked at themselves) as better than others, they would not escape punishment. This warning was to apostles and should speak loudly to that ministry today.[1]

God is not blind and He will not be mocked. If you abuse His people for whom He made you an overseer, He will punish you. If you abuse offerings, destroy unity in the church by not embracing the whole body of Christ, or cut your people out of the flow of the Holy Spirit like Diotrephes (3 John 9–10) did, and/or try to build your own kingdom, remember these warnings—you are in trouble. Jesus threatened Peter, James, John, and the other nine with this, and He does not love you any more than those. You can pretty well count on Judas being in Gehenna, and Peter might have ended up there too, if Jesus had not confronted him (John 21:15–17) at the "fish fry" and had him confess Him three times to eradicate his prior denials.

Look at what Jesus said to the scribes and Pharisees, the religious leaders of His day and time.

> *Woe unto you, scribes and Pharisees, hypocrites! for ye compass sea and land to make one proselyte, and when he is made, ye make him twofold more the child of hell [Gehenna] than yourselves.   Matthew 23:15*
>
> *Ye serpents, ye generation of vipers, how can ye escape the damnation of hell [Gehenna]?*
>   *Matthew 23:33*

This is pointedly directed to leaders—those who were given responsibility to shepherd God's people.

> *But and if that evil servant shall say in his heart, My lord delayeth his coming; And shall begin to smite his fellowservants, and to eat and drink with the drunken; The lord of that servant shall come in a day when he looketh not for him, and in an hour that he is not aware of, And shall cut him asunder, and appoint him his portion with the hypocrites: there shall be weeping and gnashing of teeth.*
>   *Matthew 24:48–51*

In chapter 12 we uncovered some parallels between the children of Israel and the church on the way to the Promised Land/millennial kingdom. There is a type of Gehenna that is revealed in those travels, too. It deals with a man named Korah.

Korah was a leader. He gathered 250 men together and challenged Moses. He corrupted the people, and God was not pleased. We find this account in Numbers chapter 16.

> *And the earth opened her mouth, and swallowed them up, and their houses, and all the men that appertained unto Korah, and all their goods. They, and all that appertained to them, went down alive into the pit, and the earth closed upon them: and they perished from among the congregation.*
> *Numbers 16:32–33*

Now watch the fire, relative to Gehenna.

> *And there came out a fire from the LORD, and consumed the two hundred and fifty men that offered incense.* *Numbers 16:35*

It was one thing for Korah to challenge Moses, but when he took the others astray along with him, the wrath of God was kindled. This profile should show us that God will not be mocked.

Fear Him

> *And I say unto you my friends, Be not afraid of them that kill the body, and after that have no more that they can do. But I will forewarn you whom ye shall fear: Fear him, which after he hath killed hath power to cast into hell [Gehenna]; yea, I say unto you, Fear him.*
> *Luke 12:4–5*

I wonder what effect it would have upon people if they fully grasped the reality of Gehenna. Not too long ago, I read Mary Baxter's book, *The Divine Revelation of Hell*. It is intended to be, and is, a very scary book. I wonder if she has had a divine revelation of Gehenna or if she, like most people, makes them the same place. She had a revelation of a minister burning. More than likely, since most revelations are allegorical, she saw him in Gehenna instead of hell. The bad news for all ministers is that fire is just as hot in Gehenna as it is in hell. The good news is that Gehenna is durational, but hell is eternal.

Gehenna—For Those Who Destroy the Temple

Earlier we covered the verses in 1 Corinthians 3 concerning rewards at the judgment seat of Christ, but there is more to it when it comes to Gehenna.

> *Every man's work shall be made manifest: for the day shall declare it, because it shall be revealed by fire; and the fire shall try every man's work of what sort it is. If any man's work abide which he hath built thereupon, he shall receive a reward. If any man's work shall be burned, he shall suffer loss: but he himself shall be saved; yet so as by fire.*
> *1 Corinthians 3:13–15*

We will all be tested by fire. Those who work and build good things on the proper foundation will be rewarded. But those who destroy what they were sent to build will be punished.

> *Know ye [plural] not that ye are the temple of God, and that the Spirit of God dwelleth in you? If any man defile the temple [the church] of God, him shall God destroy; for the temple of God is holy, which temple ye are.*
> *1 Corinthians 3:16–17*

These verses are often used to tell people not to defile their physical bodies. Hey, that is a good idea too, and there are other verses to corroborate that truth, but these verses are speaking about the whole temple of the body of Christ. God will punish those individuals who were supposed to be busy building the body of Christ, but destroyed it instead.

How Long Will Gehenna Last?

The answer to this question is not specifically stated in the Bible, but the Scriptures do say "one day with the Lord is as a thousand years." (See 2 Peter 3:8.) There are verses in the Bible that talk about burning during the day of the Lord.

> *For, behold, the day cometh, that shall burn as an oven; and all the proud, yea, and all that do wickedly, shall be stubble: and the day that cometh shall burn them up, saith the LORD of hosts, that it shall leave them neither root nor branch.* Malachi 4:1

Isaiah 10 has details about that day, the 1,000-year reign, or the seventh day of the week of millennia.

> *Therefore shall the Lord, the Lord of hosts, send among his fat ones leanness; and under his glory he shall kindle a burning like the burning of a fire. And the light of Israel shall be for a fire, and his Holy One for a flame: and it shall burn and devour his thorns and his briers in one day.* Isaiah 10:16–17

Verse 18 shows that this is not talking about burning bushes or thorns and briers. Notice the usage of the words "his," "soul and body," and "they."

> *And shall consume the glory of his forest, and of his fruitful field, both soul and body: and they shall be as when a standardbearer fainteth.* Isaiah 10:18

When it says, "they shall be as when a standardbearer fainteth," a deeper meaning is indicated. This refers to those who will be the leaders and the ones to whom others looked for direction. It is sad, but God wants His people to know that

He will not be mocked, and He has a punishment in store for those who abuse His people.

There are other verses that relate to the punishment of corrupt leaders within the church. Some of these seem to refer to the Outer Darkness. Only the Lord has the right to sentence someone to either of these places. Our concern is to understand that these places do exist and to see that we do not go there.

> *Raging waves of the sea, foaming out their own shame; wandering stars, to whom is reserved the blackness of darkness for ever.*
> *Jude 1:13*

> *These are wells without water, clouds that are carried with a tempest; to whom the mist of darkness is reserved for ever.   2 Peter 2:17*

These verses both involve the words "for ever." This phrase can be quite misleading, and therefore, I have devoted an appendix to its study (appendix F, "The Word 'Eternal'"). This phrase actually means "for an age" and, in this case, it means the age of Jesus' 1,000-year reign.

Is Gehenna Just for Leaders?

Perhaps you are wondering if Gehenna is just for leaders. The answer to this question is clearly no! It is for all those who know the truth well and then walk away from it. Hebrews 6:4 begins talking about people who are born again and have tasted of the heavenly gift and have become fully indoctrinated with the things of the Word of God.

> *For it is impossible for those who were once enlightened, and have tasted of the heavenly gift, and were made partakers of the Holy Ghost.   Hebrews 6:4*

The conclusion of this section is that those who never return again to God could well spend some time in punishment, not just in time out.

> *But that which beareth thorns and briers is rejected, and is nigh unto cursing; whose end is to be burned.* Hebrews 6:8

Another verse that shows the danger of Gehenna for all believers, not just leaders, is James 3:6.

> *And the tongue [which every believer has] is a fire, a world of iniquity: so is the tongue among our members [of the church], that it defileth the whole body [of Christ], and setteth on fire the course of nature; and it is set on fire of hell [Gehenna].* James 3:6

Gossips and talebearers, beware. You are not exempt. If you defile the body of Christ with your words, God will hold you accountable.

If these words frighten you, then they have made their mark. I am doing my job. Fear is good, because it will keep you out of Gehenna.

> *And others save with fear, pulling them out of the fire; hating even the garment spotted by the flesh.* Jude 1:23

Some people will not receive loving reproof; they must be rebuked and shown the consequences of disobedience. Hebrews 6:9 says, "beloved we are persuaded better things of you" and I am of you, too. Perhaps someone you know may need these words, and I hope and pray that we all have the heart and good sense to listen. May we all be saved with fear and pulled out of the fire of Gehenna.

Be not deceived; God is not mocked. Even though we have been saved by grace and have the hope of eternal life in the new heavens and earth, the millennial kingdom is still "up for grabs." We will all go to the judgment seat of Christ. Some will go into the 1,000-year reign of Jesus on the earth. Some will go into the Outer Darkness, and others will go into Gehenna.

May the encouraging words of Hebrews 6:10–12 be the holy benediction spoken over you.

> *For God is not unrighteous to forget your work and labour of love, which ye have shewed toward his name, in that ye have ministered to the saints, and do minister. And we desire that every one of you do shew the same diligence to the full assurance of hope unto the end: That ye be not slothful, but followers of them who through faith and patience inherit the promises.*   *Hebrews 6:10–12*

CHAPTER 17
THE CLOSE OF THE KINGDOM

Without a doubt, there *is* a close to the millennial reign of Jesus on the earth.

> *And I saw an angel come down from heaven, having the key of the bottomless pit and a great chain in his hand. And he laid hold on the dragon, that old serpent, which is the Devil, and Satan, and bound him a thousand years, And cast him into the bottomless pit, and shut him up, and set a seal upon him, that he should deceive the nations no more, till the thousand years should be fulfilled: and after that he must be loosed a little season. And I saw thrones, and they sat upon them, and judgment was given unto them: and I saw the souls of them that were beheaded for the witness of Jesus, and for the word of God, and which had not worshipped the beast, neither his image, neither had received his mark upon their foreheads, or in their hands; and they lived and reigned with Christ a thousand years. But the rest of the dead lived not again until the thousand years were finished. This is the first resurrection. Blessed and holy is he*

> *that hath part in the first resurrection: on such the second death hath no power, but they shall be priests of God and of Christ, and shall reign with him a thousand years. And when the thousand years are expired, Satan shall be loosed out of his prison.*   Revelation 20:1–7

At the close of this age God will allow Satan to be loosed to try those who will have been living on the earth during that era. There will be a major deception before God destroys Satan with fire coming down from heaven and then throws him in the lake of fire and seals his fate for ever and ever.

> *And shall go out to deceive the nations which are in the four quarters of the earth, Gog, and Magog, to gather them together to battle: the number of whom is as the sand of the sea. And they went up on the breadth of the earth, and compassed the camp of the saints about, and the beloved city: and fire came down from God out of heaven, and devoured them. And the devil that deceived them was cast into the lake of fire and brimstone, where the beast and the false prophet are, and shall be tormented day and night for ever and ever.*
>   Revelation 20:8–10

The concluding verses of Revelation 20 finish with the great white throne judgment, where the dead, both small and great are judged. This is not the judgment seat of Christ, since that happened at the beginning of Jesus' millennial kingdom. This is the end of the seventh day of the week of millennia. Then the events of the new heavens and earth and the eternal kingdom of the Father begin to unfold.

> *And I saw a new heaven and a new earth: for the first [former] heaven and the first [former] earth were passed away; and there was no more sea.*   Revelation 21:1

The Close of the Kingdom

All of the events of the former (second) heavens and earth conclude with Jesus putting down the final rebellion from Satan and casting him into the lake of fire. This is the "end" that 1 Corinthians 15:24 details.

> *Then cometh the end, when he [Jesus Christ] shall have delivered up the kingdom to God, even the Father; when he shall have put down all rule and all authority and power.*
> *1 Corinthians 15:24*

The end that verse 25 covers is the end of Jesus' millennial kingdom.

> *For he [Jesus] must reign [in His kingdom], till he hath put all enemies under his feet. The last enemy that shall be destroyed is death.*
> *1 Corinthians 15:25–26*

Death is destroyed when it is cast into the lake of fire from Revelation 20:14. Now pay close attention to the next two verses from 1 Corinthians 15. They reveal the end of the millennial reign when Jesus delivers the whole kingdom of the earth to His Father in order for the kingdom of the Father to begin.

> *For he [God the Father] hath put all things under his [Jesus Christ's] feet. But when he [God the Father] saith all things are put under him [Jesus Christ], it is manifest [obvious] that he [God the Father] is excepted, which did put all things under him [Jesus Christ]. And when all things shall be subdued unto him [Jesus Christ], then shall the Son also himself be subject unto him [God the Father] that put all things under him [Jesus Christ], that God [the Father] may be all in all.*
> *1 Corinthians 15:27–28*

Since Jesus puts down the last rebellion, He must then gather those in the Outer Darkness and Gehenna and bring them together with the believers who will have been reigning with Him on earth. Revelation 20:15 indicates that there were some who came out of the dead (not alive in bodies) who are not cast into the lake of fire.

> *And whosoever was not found written in the book of life was cast into the lake of fire.*
> *Revelation 20:15*

These are the ones Jesus will reunite together in one and deliver to the Father in order for the kingdom of the Father to begin. Look at this verse in Ephesians 1:10. It is a mystery to most people until they realize the full truth of what Jesus is going to put back together.

> *That in the dispensation [administration] of the fulness of times [not time] he might gather together in one all things in Christ, both which are in heaven [those left in the Outer Darkness and in Gehenna], and which are on earth [reigning with Jesus in His kingdom]; even in him.*
> *Ephesians 1:10*

This verse has been an enigma to many people for a long, long time. The best explanation has been that this refers to the rapture of the church, but that cannot be, since there will be many, many more people saved upon the earth after the rapture of the church. Others say that this will transpire in the administration of the fullness of times (plural). The fullness of times will not occur until after the millennial kingdom concludes.

The Lord will take those who have been languishing in the Outer Darkness and those who have been punished in Gehenna and put them together with those who have been reigning with Him on the earth and present them to the Father. He will say (pardon the license of conjecture),

The Close of the Kingdom

"Father, here are the ones who have believed in You and Me. These are the ones who have reigned with Me and those who have learned their lessons. They are all Your children by grace, because they have believed on Me."

Now look at the explanation of Ephesians 1:11–14. It makes sense now.

> *In whom also we [all, both from the heavens and off of the earth] have obtained an inheritance [of grace for the kingdom of the Father], being predestinated according to the purpose of him [God the Father] who worketh all things after the counsel of his own will: That we should be to the praise of his glory, who first trusted in Christ. In whom ye also trusted, after that ye heard the word of truth, the gospel of your salvation [of your spirit by grace]: in whom also after that ye believed [the key to receiving the gospel of grace], ye were sealed with that holy Spirit of promise, Which is the earnest [the token] of our inheritance [of grace] until the redemption of the purchased possession [both those in heaven and on earth], unto the praise of his glory.*   *Ephesians 1:11–14*

While in Bible college I personally studied Ephesians until I had memorized the whole book; but I never understood these verses until I realized that in the fullness of times Jesus would gather all those in heaven (those who were waiting for the millennial kingdom to conclude) with those on earth (those reigning with Him) to present them to the Father so that the kingdom of the Father could begin.

In Revelation 21:1–7, we read John's account of a great voice from heaven speaking to all those coming out of the Outer Darkness, Gehenna, and the millennial kingdom.

> *And I saw a new heaven and a new earth: for the first heaven and the first earth were passed away; and there was no more sea. And I John saw the holy city, new Jerusalem, coming down from God out of heaven, prepared as a bride adorned for her husband. And I heard a great voice out of heaven saying, Behold, the tabernacle of God [the Father] is with men, and he will dwell with them, and they shall be his people, and God [the Father] himself shall be with them, and be their God [and Father]. And God [the Father] shall wipe away all tears from their eyes; and there shall be no more death, neither sorrow, nor crying, neither shall there be any more pain: for the former things are passed away. And he that sat upon the throne said, Behold, I make all things new. And he said unto me, Write: for these words are true and faithful. And he said unto me, It is done. I am Alpha and Omega, the beginning and the end. I will give unto him that is athirst of the fountain of the water of life freely. He that overcometh shall inherit all things; and I will be his God, and he shall be my son.*
> Revelation 21:1–7

This is the beginning of the kingdom of the Father, where all His sons and daughters who have believed on Him will now live with Him. Everyone will have been purged. The Outer Darkness will be over, as well as Gehenna. Look closely at verse 4 again.

> *And God [the Father] shall wipe away all tears from their eyes; and there shall be no more death [it will have been cast into the lake of fire], neither sorrow [of separation from Jesus], nor crying [weeping], neither shall*

> *there be any more pain [from Gehenna] for the former things [of the second heavens and earth] are passed away.*   Revelation 21:4

This will be the close of the second heavens and earth and the beginning of the kingdom of God the Father. All of those who have believed in Jesus will now overcome, and they will have God as their Father. He will be their God, and they will be His sons.

Conclusion

After this extensive study concerning the 1,000-year reign of Jesus on the earth, there are a number of salient points that we want to reiterate and always hold onto.

Never forget that there are two gospels and two inheritances. Let no man deceive you. If you have embraced Jesus Christ as your Savior and Lord, God the Father has graciously given you the inheritance of the new heavens and earth. This is your gift from your Father, Who is no respecter of persons.

Next, you have the right as a child of God to prove yourself worthy to reign with Jesus and receive the inheritance of reward, which is the millennial reign of Jesus on the earth. You will need to serve Him as a good and faithful servant all the days of your life and present your body as a living sacrifice to Him as you are led by the Holy Spirit.

There *is* such a place as the Outer Darkness. The depth of what you want to know about it is that you *do not* want to go there and spend the reign of Jesus on the earth in the heavens doing a time out in order to figure out what you should have figured out while living on the earth. There is also a place called Gehenna for apostate and rebellious children of God. It is a place of punishment.

We thank God the Father for His mercy and goodness to make us heirs of His kingdom and for giving us the right to prove ourselves worthy for the reign of Jesus on the earth. Perhaps more than any other section of Scripture, the one that summarizes the truths we have studied is the old Christian hymn of the early church. It spoke to them and it will speak to us.

> *This is a faithful saying: For if we died with Him, we shall also live with Him. If we endure, we shall also reign with Him. If we deny Him, He also will deny us. If we are faithless, He remains faithful; He cannot deny Himself.*
> *2 Timothy 2:11–13 NKJ*

May we all be so fortunate as to stand before the Lord and hear:

> *"His lord said to him, 'Well done, good and faithful servant; you were faithful over a few things, I will make you ruler over many things. Enter into the joy of your lord.'"*
> *Matthew 25:21*

APPENDIXES

Having taught this class publicly for quite a few years, I have become acquainted with frequently asked questions and have included the following appendixes to help answer questions that may arise. The purpose of these collateral materials is to augment your study of Jesus' millennial kingdom. These topics are closely related to the focal subject but could be left out without missing any fundamental truths.

> Appendix A—**The Woman Who Hid the Kingdom** is an item of great interest to individuals who desire more information on how we lost the truths of the millennial kingdom.

> Appendix B—**The Kingdom of God and the Kingdom of Heaven** is a study that will help you grasp the correlation between these descriptive phrases and help you to understand why they are at times used interchangeably.

Appendix C—**Can You Lose Your Salvation?** is closely related to the 1,000-year reign of Jesus on the earth because the salvation of your soul, which you *can* lose, will cost you the millennial kingdom, but the salvation of the spirit, which is by grace, you *cannot* lose and it gives you the inheritance of grace and the new heavens and earth.

Appendix D—**Life in the Millennial Kingdom** contains research in an organized manner to offer some answers from the Bible on what to expect in the coming kingdom.

Appendix E—**Rewards in the Kingdom of the Father** will show the triple indemnity ensuing from faithfully serving the Lord now. It reveals that rewards given to the bride in the kingdom of heaven will carry over into the kingdom of the Father.

Appendix F—**The Word "Eternal"** covers the definition of the Greek word *aion* and exposes erroneous translations which suggest the millennial kingdom will last forever.

Appendix G—**Matthew 24:14** provides a detailed explanation of the future prophetic fulfilment of this verse.

APPENDIX A
THE WOMAN WHO HID THE KINGDOM

Since we have already laid a foundation of understanding concerning the kingdom of heaven and have learned about the sufferings and glory of the Lord, we are prepared to look at a tremendously deep and yet very revealing aspect concerning the "hiding" of the kingdom of heaven. This comes from a series of parables in Matthew 13 spoken by Jesus the Prophet. When viewed as a whole, we will develop a picture of this woman, whom we will see is the queen of heaven, hiding the kingdom of heaven in an attempt to replace Jesus Christ as the believers' true intercessor and to hide the reality of His coming kingdom. Be forewarned that this chapter goes deep into the background of the promised reign of Jesus on the earth—it not only holds tremendous potential for understanding, but also could be offensive to the kingdoms of the world and to those whom the queen of heaven has deceived.

Jesus prophesied through eight parables in Matthew 13 that the kingdom of heaven would come under great siege. In the first four parables, He foretold that this great truth would be lost; in the next three, Jesus revealed it would be regained;

and in the final one, He told us how to understand it. (It is possible that this book, along with other materials of this sort, could very well be a part of that prophesied fulfillment of this rediscovered truth.) We are heading down the corridor of end-time fulfillment and must be prepared to go to battle with the enemy who has hidden this truth if we are to regain it and ultimately derive the profit of commitment that it will inure.

We will of necessity retrace some historical facts to discover how this woman hid the kingdom. Since 60 percent of church history occurred during the Roman Catholic Church's undisputed leadership (and over 85 percent of it during its existence), it is inevitable that some of this information will deal with that institution and the losses that were incurred during its time of control. We will see the emergence of the queen of heaven into its belief system and the resulting consequence of the kingdom of heaven being lost. Some of this may be unsettling and may seem somewhat controversial, but as in all excavation work, the rubble must be moved and sorted to find the treasure lying beneath the surface. May we all realize that the confusion and loss of understanding of the 1,000-year reign of Jesus on the earth has been attributed to what Jesus said, "An enemy has done this." Our enemy is the devil, and he has made victims of all those in his path, both Roman Catholics and other Christians alike.

The Prophecy of Jesus

In the series of eight parables in Matthew 13, Jesus, in the Prophet's role, disclosed that the kingdom of heaven would be under violent siege and that the understanding of it would be lost. Understanding these parables will give us insight into the mysteries of the kingdom of heaven. There are deeper meanings than "meet the eye," which prophetically predicted

Appendix A

the loss of what we are now trying to recover. Notice that in *all* of the parables, Jesus proclaimed, "The kingdom of heaven is like . . ." This shows that all eight parables deal with the same subject and provide insight into the coming 1,000-year reign on the earth.

Jesus first began using parables in Matthew 13. When His disciples asked Him why He used them, Jesus said it was *to hide truth that was relevant to others*. This reveals a great fact to us that is still concealed from much of Christianity—**parables are hidden truths that were reserved for the coming church age**. Although Jesus spoke them to Israel, they were addressed to the church that would come later. By the time of Matthew 13, it was apparent to Jesus that the Jewish nation was going to reject Him (12:14). They had already imprisoned John the Baptist (chapter 11), and Jesus had begun to turn the kingdom building over to the Gentiles (12:18). By Matthew 13, Jesus starts teaching parables that only the church would eventually understand. These truths are relative to the mystery period (see chapter 5, "The Sufferings and the Glory of the Lord") and were specifically addressed to those who would be alive during that era. These secrets had been kept (like the mystery of Romans 16:25; 1 Corinthians 2:7–8; and Ephesians 3:4–6) since the foundations of the world.

> *All these things spake Jesus unto the multitude in parables; and without a parable spake he not unto them: That it might be fulfilled which was spoken by the prophet, saying, I will open my mouth in parables;* ***I will utter things which have been kept secret from the foundation of the world.***
> *Matthew 13:34–35*

It is within these parables that Jesus prophesied the kingdom of heaven would be lost during this present period of the church of the body of Christ—between the sufferings and the glory of the Lord. The parables provide vital insight to those of the church who would much later read these verses.

> *And the disciples came, and said unto him, Why speakest thou unto them in parables? He answered and said unto them,* ***Because it is given unto you*** *[who believe in me]* ***to know the mysteries of the kingdom of heaven****, but to them [who reject me] it is not given.*   *Matthew 13:10–11*

Our primary focus will be on the *fourth parable*, in which the woman hides the kingdom of heaven in three measures of meal. However, a brief synopsis of each of the parables will show the depth of the deception and the focused efforts of the devil to obscure this kingdom. This is necessary to observe, since there is a flow to all these parables, and the context must be understood in order to grasp the whole picture. The first four parables dealing with wheat and the seed of the kingdom show the impending threat of loss of the kingdom. The next three show how to regain it, and the last one reveals to us the value of the kingdom that has been lost.

> **Parable #1:** In the parable of the sower (Matthew 13:3–9, 18–23), Jesus said that the seed of the kingdom would suffer severe tests in bringing forth fruit unto the kingdom of heaven. (This cannot pertain to the gospel of grace, because the gospel of grace is for eternal life and it could never be lost.)
>
> **Parable #2:** In the parable of the tares (Matthew 13:24–30, 37–43), Jesus said that an enemy would sow tares among the wheat and that at the end of the age they would be sorted out. (This parable shows that there are children of the devil masquerading as children of God within the church, and that they are major opponents to the 1,000-year reign.)

Appendix A

Parable #3: In the parable of the mustard plant (Matthew 13:31–32), Jesus predicted the sowing of a mustard seed in the same field (His field) where the wheat was sown. This shows a little seed that is sown among the wheat but grows up and sticks out like a sore thumb as a big tree right in the middle of a wheat field. The tree would overshadow the rest of the wheat field to the point that birds (representative of demons) would nest in it and eat the seeds of the kingdom (13:4, 19). (This parable reveals that a giant perversion or heresy would arise among the whole church that would become a nesting place for those who would consume the seeds of the kingdom.)

Parable #4: In the parable of the leaven in the three measures of meal (13:33), Jesus foretold that *doctrine* (leaven) would be hidden in three measures of milled seeds from the field until all of it was corrupted by false doctrine (concerning the kingdom of heaven). He was specific to foretell that a "woman" would hide the leaven (false doctrine).

Notice that the first four parables were taught publicly by the seaside (Matthew 13:1). Jesus went *out of* the house to teach them. These four parables were taught *publicly* to reveal the prophetic significance of parables and how the kingdom of heaven would be lost. These four started with seeds being sown and finally finished with leaven being sown among the milled seeds that were harvested. After sharing the first four parables, Jesus sent the multitude away and went into the house, where He could have intimacy of fellowship with those who believed on him. After going into the house, He began explaining the parable of the wheat and tares. After giving the interpretation of the parable of the tares, He then shared four more parables. The next three reveal what we must do to *recover* what would be lost.

Parable #5: In the parable of the treasure (13:44), we see that when the kingdom of heaven is recovered from where it has been hidden, then we must sell all we have to get it. (Notice that it was *hidden*.)

Parable #6: The parable of the pearl (13:45) shows that when the kingdom of heaven (the 1,000-year reign of Jesus) is rediscovered then we must sell all we have to acquire this one treasure. (Notice that he had to *find* it.)

Parable #7: In the parable of the drag net (13:47–50), Jesus showed the end-time harvest and the coming of the kingdom when the church would be sorted (judged) at the judgment seat of Christ (Matthew 22 and 2 Corinthians 5:10). This judgment will be between those who have been good enough to enter the kingdom of heaven (see chapter 7, "The Bride Comes Out of the Body") and those who will be cast into the Outer Darkness (see chapter 15, "The Outer Darkness"). This parable reveals the reward for those who discover the kingdom and pay the price to find it, obtain it, and keep it.

After Jesus conveyed these three parables concerning the recovery of the kingdom, He asked His disciples if they understood what He had said. They responded, "Yea, Lord." Actually, they did not have a clue and He knew this, so He concluded with the final parable that is specifically addressed to those (including us) who would read it during this age of grace.

Parable #8: In the parable of the scribe (13:52), Jesus instructs what every scribe (anyone learned in the law, or those studying according to the instructions in 2 Peter 3:15 and 16) must do in order to understand the kingdom of heaven. They (we) must *bring out the treasures of the old* (the suffering) *and* *the new* (the coming glory). We must bring out all the old treasures of understanding of the suffering and crucifixion of the Lord and set them alongside the new treasures about the coming glory of the kingdom of heaven and the 1,000-year reign of Jesus on the earth. To fully understand the kingdom of heaven, we must compare the past suffering and the coming glory.

Even though this has been a lengthy exposé of the parables of Matthew 13, we have seen the prophetic words of Jesus—*that this truth would be lost and that we must be willing to give everything to regain it.* We must press into this topic even further to learn about the inheritances we have. This will unfold unto us as we explore the fourth parable of Matthew 13—the parable of the leaven in the three measures of meal.

The Leaven in the Three Measures of Meal

To properly understand this parable, we have had to study all the others. We must remember that the fourth one is set in the middle of the package of eight and cannot be lifted out of its context. It falls at the end of the first group of four, where we see the culmination of the deception that hid the truth of the millennial reign of Jesus on the earth.

The scope of the first four parables is *the loss of the kingdom*. The story line is all about the seed of the gospel of the kingdom of heaven—not the gospel of grace. It begins with the seed not bringing forth fruit because it was eaten by the wayside or scorched or choked. The seed that survived and brought forth fruit was mingled with the tares sown among them. Then a giant tree would spring up in the middle of the field, housing birds that would eat the seeds produced.

In following the flow of these parables, we find that even after the wheat seed (of the kingdom) has survived the scorching of the sun, choking of the thorns, growing among the tares, and the ravenous birds that dwelt in the midst of the field, some are finally harvested. Then after the wheat was harvested, it was "milled" into meal. This is precious insight, because even those who survived the onslaught of deception, and had produced fruit for the kingdom, would *all* finally be deceived by a woman leavening the whole harvested lot. In other words, *the whole church was going to become corrupted* and deceived by this "woman."

Now the kingdom of heaven is likened unto leaven which a "woman" will hide in three separate measures of meal. Unmistakably, leaven is used in Scripture to reference false doctrine that totally spreads like it has a mind of its own. It corrupts everything it touches.

> *Then understood they how that he bade them not beware of the leaven of bread, but of the doctrine of the Pharisees and of the Sadducees.*
> *Matthew 16:12*

Mark 8:15 and Luke 12:1 relate the same truth, so when we read that a woman puts leaven into three measures of meal, it means that the thirty-, sixty- or hundredfold (threefold measures) who brought forth fruit, will now have false doctrine spread throughout them until all of the church is blinded to the kingdom of heaven.

The Woman

At this point we must reckon that the woman is not a good character, because she is trying to destroy the kingdom of heaven. This is not the bride of Christ; to the contrary, it is the "other" woman of biblical prophecy—the *harlot, Mystery Babylon*. **This is not the bride of Christ, but the queen of heaven** (Jeremiah 7:18, 44:17–19 and 25).

The way we know that the woman is the queen of heaven is a matter of simple deduction. From the entire scope of Scripture dealing with the kingdom of heaven there are only

Appendix A

two possibilities of who she could be. Since the kingdom of heaven deals with world rulership and unfolding prophetic events of world rulership, we know that the woman must be either the bride of Christ or the mother of harlots (Revelation 17:3–5, 18:23), the queen of heaven.

Knowing that the woman is hiding leaven (false doctrine) in the meal, we intuitively deduce that the woman is the queen of heaven. It is the nature of this doctrine that we must understand in order to regain the lost kingdom.

Because we know the prophesied promise that the bride of Christ is to reign with Jesus during the 1,000-year period, we can see what the queen of heaven has been trying to do. She tried to hide the bride of Christ and the promised rulership with Jesus by building her own kingdom and world rulership, attempting to cloak the coming reign of Jesus Christ and His bride.

Look at the two women at the end of time—just before the reign of Jesus.

> *And upon her forehead was a name written, MYSTERY, BABYLON THE GREAT, THE MOTHER OF HARLOTS AND ABOMINATIONS OF THE EARTH.* Revelation 17:5

> *Let us be glad and rejoice, and give honour to him: for the marriage of the Lamb is come, and his wife hath made herself ready. And to her was granted that she should be arrayed in fine linen, clean and white: for the fine linen is the righteousness of saints.*
> Revelation 19:7–8

What the queen of heaven has been trying to hide is the promised reign of Jesus on the earth. She has been trying to implement her own world order, government, and kingdom in order to obscure the reality of the bride of Christ.

The woman who hid the kingdom of heaven was trying to superimpose the lie of her kingdom (Mystery Babylon) over that of the reign of the Lord's bride with the true King of heaven during the 1,000-year reign of Jesus on this earth.

We find references to the queen of heaven throughout Scripture. Wherever you see her, she is trying to set up a world empire in order to hide the prophesied reign of Jesus on the earth. The mention of her by name comes from Jeremiah 7:18, 44:17–19 and 25. This was during a period of time just prior to the children of Israel (the kingdom of Judah) going into captivity in Babylon. Look at the worship given her.

> *Seest thou not what they do in the cities of Judah and in the streets of Jerusalem? The children gather wood, and the fathers kindle the fire, and the women knead their dough,* **to make cakes to the queen of heaven**, *and to pour out drink offerings unto other gods, that they may provoke me to anger.*
> *Jeremiah 7: 17–18*

The making of cakes is another reference that ties the woman who hid leaven in the three measures of meal (Matthew 13:33) to the queen of heaven (Jeremiah 7:17–18 and 44:19). In other words, the milled seeds or flour used to make cakes is where the woman hid the false doctrine to hide the kingdom of heaven and the reign of Jesus on the earth. As a result, those who thought they were genuinely worshiping the King of glory would, in fact, be worshiping the queen of heaven.

Because they worshiped her, God sent Israel and Judah into captivity. While in captivity, God showed the king of Babylon, Nebuchadnezzar, a dream about the kingdoms of the world that would reign over Israel. Understanding this dream will show us why the "woman" or queen of

Appendix A

heaven is finally referred to as MYSTERY BABYLON, *the mother of all harlots.*

The dream of Nebuchadnezzar was about a huge statue that represented world rulership and its domination over the children of Israel. In fact, as we now see the truth revealed in Revelation 17:5, it illustrated the effect and rulership of the queen of heaven in the world. This dream, interpreted by Daniel, showed the kingdoms of the world beginning in Babylon. Then the mother of harlots passed the lie down to Persia, then to Greece, and finally to Rome. The queen of heaven moved right along through all the world powers, if not being the dominant force that brought each one to power. It is well documented through history that these in fact were the subsequent world powers. The power granted to them was spiritually transmitted through the principality of the queen of heaven. She has played a major role in all of these kingdoms. Each of these kingdoms has stood as the world leader of its time and was the substitute for one-world government—a counterfeit of what Jesus will establish.

The truth that the queen of heaven has been trying to hide is the culmination of the dream interpreted by Daniel. *It is the coming judgment upon her and the kingdoms of the world*. She has been trying to hide the prophesied truth of Daniel 2:44.

> *And in the days of these kings shall the God of heaven set up a kingdom, which shall never be destroyed: and the kingdom shall not be left to other people, but it shall break in pieces and consume all these kingdoms, and it shall stand for ever.*   Daniel 2:44

The queen of heaven has held her position in all of these kingdoms. In Babylon, she ruled under the name of Semiramis;[1] in Persia, she was Pinikir;[2] in Greece, she was Aphrodite;[3] and in Rome, she was Venus.[4] This is the same spirit personality but with different names in different cultures/kingdoms of the world. During both Greek and Roman rule, she also adopted the name Diana. Regardless of the name used, this is still the queen of heaven. Acts 19:27 references worship directed toward her.

> *So that not only this our craft is in danger to be set at nought; but also that the temple of the great goddess **Diana** should be despised, and her magnificence should be destroyed, **whom all Asia and the world worshippeth**.*
> *Acts 19:27*

As revealing as these truths are, the final hiding place for the queen of heaven was not just within the Roman Empire, but in the *religion* of the Roman Empire—the Roman Catholic Church. As church history records, the Roman Catholic Church took control of *the* church in A.D. 325 at the Council of Nicea. It was at this time that the queen of heaven buried herself within the syncretism of Roman Catholic traditions being mixed with pagan practices. *When she emerged she was not Venus or Diana, but Mary the Mother of God.* Operating under this name did not change her intentions. She has always tried to hide the fact that there is a coming King and kingdom that will crush her.

As the queen of heaven hid herself under the name of the beautiful mother of Jesus, she showed her true colors by causing all to look at *her* instead of the true object of Christianity—Jesus Christ. She leavened the doctrine of the kingdom of heaven and hid the truth of the threefold ministry of Jesus Christ: Prophet, Priest, and King. She stole His worship, His importance, and the knowledge of His coming kingdom.

Appendix A

The Three Measures of Meal

What the three measures of meal represent is very important to this subject of the gospel of the kingdom. This is vital, especially if we are going to recover the commitment that has been lost due to hiding the kingdom of heaven. Although the meaning of the three measures of meal is subjectively interpreted, the metaphor, however, *must* represent something relative to the kingdom of heaven, and it must tie in closely with the queen of heaven. Now that we have come to the parable dealing with the three measures of meal, we can document without a doubt that the woman is the queen of heaven. Look at the correspondence of what Jesus said to Jeremiah's reference to the worship of the queen of heaven by making cakes.

> *And when we burned incense to the queen of heaven, and poured out drink offerings unto her,* **did we make her cakes to worship her**, *and pour out drink offerings unto her, without our men?* Jeremiah 44:19

The parable in Matthew 13:33 is undoubtedly a reference to the queen of heaven. What the three measures of meal represent is more that just the thirty-, sixty-, hundredfold seed produced; it is the intermingling of *leaven* and *false doctrine*. This is a matter of **great** importance since it is the fourth and final parable in the progression of how and where the kingdom of heaven was hidden. What the three measures of meal represent shows how and under what false doctrine the kingdom of heaven was hidden.

There are a number of possibilities for what the three measures represent. Some have supposed that three parts represent Persia, Greece, and Rome. This docs have some validity, since each of these three kingdoms furthered the mystery of Babylon and the presence of the queen of heaven, but these existed before the age of the church—to whom the parable was addressed. Others have postulated that it is the doctrine of the trinity. This also has some merit for consideration, since most Christians do not separate the Father, Son, and Holy Spirit and subsequently do not realize that each has a portion of the kingdom of God over which He presides. (See appendix B, "The Kingdom of God and the Kingdom of Heaven".)

Perhaps the most intriguing and credible explanation involves the mingling and hiding of the threefold ministry of Jesus Christ as Prophet, Priest, and King. This conceivably is the most plausible, since it obscures the present ministry of Jesus as High Priest and Intercessor and the *future* ministry of Jesus on the earth as the King of glory. This was, still is, and will be, the ploy of the queen of heaven—to steal worship and hide the prophecy of the coming *glory* of the King on the earth. Posing as the ruler of a one-world government, she also positions herself to fulfill end-time prophecy as the woman riding upon and directing the final world power that the Lord will destroy when He comes forth out of heaven.

Again we see the queen of heaven stripped bare before all people and the disguises of Semiramis, Pinikir, Aphrodite, Venus, Diana, or Mary the Mother of God, ripped off at her final demise. *She is the mother of all these harlots—the queen of heaven—the mother of all abominations on the earth.*

> *And upon her forehead was a name written, MYSTERY, BABYLON THE GREAT, THE MOTHER OF HARLOTS AND ABOMINATIONS OF THE EARTH.*   Revelation 17:5

She is the mother of all cults. Hidden beneath the rubble of confusion and world empires, the queen of heaven will be

Appendix A

destroyed so that the true King of glory will openly reign over the entire world.

When the queen of heaven disguised herself as Mary the Mother of God, she took the focus off the *true* central figure of Christianity—Jesus Christ—and put it upon herself. Like all of the "mystery" religions, the focus has been on the *queen* and not the true King. In focusing the attention upon herself, the queen of heaven leavened the doctrine of the church and hid the true doctrine that would reveal the kingdom of heaven. The church has missed the tri-fold ministry of Jesus Christ as Prophet, Priest, and King. Our understanding of Jesus' ministry must be reclaimed.

The Prophet, Priest, and King

When the Word of God communicates completeness, it uses packages of three. A few examples are: *Father, Son, Holy Spirit; spirit, soul, body; Moses, Aaron, Hur; Peter, James, John; three days and nights; "was, is, and is to come."* When God chose to communicate the ministry of Jesus Christ, He used the package of *Prophet, Priest,* and *King*. This is the complete depiction of Jesus' ministry to God's people.

This threefold aspect of Jesus' ministry has basically been a hidden reality, due to the queen of heaven obscuring it. If most Christians were asked: "What is Jesus' ministry now?" they would respond, "Savior." Even though He *is* the Savior of all men, this is not His *primary* function now. He is serving as the *High Priest of God, making intercession for all men in the presence of the Father.*

> *Wherefore he is able also to save them to the uttermost that come unto God by him, seeing he ever liveth to make intercession for them. For such an high priest became us, who is holy,*

> *harmless, undefiled, separate from sinners, and made higher than the heavens.*
> *Hebrews 7:25–26*

There is a method to the madness of hiding this truth about the threefold ministry of Jesus. It has accomplished a number of objectives. The queen of heaven has siphoned off the respect due to the Lord by becoming the "apparent" intercessor for people now, but her real objective was to hide the reality of Jesus' office as King, coming in glory to rule over the earth. (His prophesied rise to power will spell her certain demise, and she wants to deceive as many as possible before she is finally destroyed.)

We have already been examining the evidences of the ministry of Jesus as the prophet by studying the prophecies in Matthew 13. He came to proclaim that the kingdom of heaven had come to earth and to be the spokesman to reconcile people to God. He came to earth and lived as a meek and submissive servant for more than 30 years, waiting for His people to recognize Him and accept Him. However, His own people rejected Him and killed Him. It might appear the story stops there, but not so . . .

The Lord ascended into heaven and has been functioning as High Priest before the throne of God day and night for the past 2,000 years.

> *Wherefore in all things it behoved him to be made like unto his brethren, that he might be a merciful and faithful high priest in things pertaining to God, to make reconciliation for the sins of the people.*   *Hebrews 2:17*

If you asked most Christians what Jesus is doing right now, they would say "sitting at the right hand of God." The truth that *Jesus is making intercession before God for us now* was replaced in the early church by the "Mother of God" being the chief intercessor. It continues even until now by those who

Appendix A

pray to Mary, believing that she will go to Jesus on their behalf. This is *totally unscriptural* and removes the centrality and significance of Jesus and replaces it with that of the queen of heaven. (This is more than obvious when the rosary is prayed and the "Hail Mary" is recited 53 times versus the Lord's Prayer being used only *six* times. *In other words, there is nine times more emphasis given to the "Mother of God" than to the Son of God.*)

Documentation of this preposterous belief is given by the writings of Alphonsus Liguori, canonized in 1839 by Pope Gregory XIV. He stated that a sinner saw a spiritual picture of two ladders hanging out of heaven. When he climbed the one, trying to get into heaven, he met the angry stare of the Lord Jesus, but then climbing the other ladder, he met Mary who took him into heaven and into the presence of the Lord. The story was given to show how much easier it is to gain forgiveness through Mary than it is through Jesus Himself.[5]

This perverts the truth of Jesus being the true shepherd and the lover of our souls. The queen of heaven has blinded the minds of those who have been unknowingly "making cakes" to her. As the truth is now known, when prayers are offered to Mary, as the "supposed" Mother of God, they are not really directed to Mary, the mother of Jesus, but to the queen of heaven. This statement is *not* made to condemn Roman Catholics who pray to "Mary," but to strip away the veil of deception and to reveal that *Jesus is our High Priest and Intercessor.* **Jesus is the compassionate Savior and High Priest of our confession who knows the feelings of our infirmities and encourages us to come boldly to the throne of grace and mercy** (Hebrews 4:15–16). As obvious as the compassion and love of the Lord is, the hidden truth of Jesus coming to earth to reign as the King of glory is even more obscured.

When Martin Luther initiated the surge of reformation within the church, he got as far as *sole fide*, or "justified by faith." Neither he, nor any of his colleagues, past or present, ventured into the arena of recognizing that Jesus Christ is King and will be coming to establish His kingdom here on earth. As was mentioned before, Augustine's amillenarial theology, adopted and promoted by the Roman Catholic Church, was the perfect screen for the queen of heaven to use. This made the coming reign of Jesus a figurative concept and has, for the most part, obscured the reality that Jesus is *literally* coming to earth to set up God's kingdom and reign from Mount Zion. It is time for this truth to become known and communicated throughout the body of Christ.

> *Then the moon shall be confounded, and the sun ashamed,* **when the LORD of hosts shall reign in mount Zion**, *and in Jerusalem, and before his ancients gloriously.*
> *Isaiah 24:23*

Concerning the discussion of the queen of heaven hiding the 1,000-year reign of Jesus on the earth, as Jesus said, "An enemy hath done this." No one ever intentionally awoke one morning and said, "I think I'll get deceived today." The whole church has been deceived through the Dark, Middle, Enlightened, and Reformed Ages. We have become the victims of the queen of heaven's attack on church doctrine. Through false doctrine, she leavened the truth of the threefold ministry of Jesus and has tried to take His place. She did this to steal the glory due Him as our intercessor during the present era and has hidden the truth that He is coming to crush her world empire and rule from Mount Zion.

I make this statement because "hell hath no fury like a woman scorned," and the most vicious is the queen of heaven. Writers making such information known to the church often come under heavy fire in retaliation for revealing these truths. This is not a political statement made to criticize Roman Catholic people, because Ephesians 6:12

Appendix A

says that we do not wrestle against flesh and blood. This is an attempt to expose the devices of wickedness promulgated by the queen of heaven to hide the millennial kingdom and the reign of our Lord Jesus Christ.

Of all the subjects I have endeavored to understand and teach, this one concerning the coming reign of Jesus has had the most spiritual opposition. However, let me quickly say that it has also fostered the most positive response and deliverance. This subject, like no other, enhances commitment in the rank and file of the Christian church and army. So, I am ready to take a stand for people to know about this coming reign and decide to either "make it or miss it."

The next three parables tell us how to recover this lost truth. They tell us to sell everything we have acquired in order to obtain this treasure. It has been hidden, and when we find it, it will be the most precious truth we have. This is a 1,000-year reign with Jesus Christ Himself on the earth. This will be, "Thy Kingdom **[has]** come. Thy will **[absolutely shall]** be done on earth, as it is in heaven," (Matthew 6:10) because Jesus will be *on the earth* sitting on His Father's throne. **He will bring the will of God to pass on the earth—not with a shepherd's crook, but with a rod of iron.**

The church is now more aware of end-time prophecies than ever before, because the Holy Spirit is making preparations for the coming of the King. We are going to see that the bride of Christ will make herself ready, even in the midst of the cunning craftiness of the queen of heaven. This kingdom of heaven is a violent kingdom and those vying for it must be ready to stand and engage the enemy.

> *And from the days of John the Baptist until now the kingdom of heaven suffereth violence, and the violent take it by force.*
> *Matthew 11:12*

APPENDIX B
The Kingdom of God and the Kingdom of Heaven

This aspect of our study needs to be included as an appendix because of our general lack of understanding about the kingdom of heaven. When we read different accounts and see the same criteria expected for both the kingdom of God and the kingdom of heaven, we find need for clarification between the two. For example,

> *Then said he, Unto what is the kingdom of God like? and whereunto shall I resemble it? It is like a grain of mustard seed, which a man took, and cast into his garden; and it grew, and waxed a great tree; and the fowls of the air lodged in the branches of it.*
>
> *Luke 13:18–19*

> *Another parable put he forth unto them, saying, The kingdom of heaven is like to a grain of mustard seed, which a man took, and sowed in his field: Which indeed is the least of all seeds: but when it is grown, it is the greatest among herbs, and becometh a tree, so*

Appendix B

> *that the birds of the air come and lodge in the branches thereof.   Matthew 13:31–32*

The reason for these different names is simple: The kingdom of God is over all, from beginning throughout eternity, but the kingdom of heaven is particular to the reign of Jesus on the earth. As simple as this is, the kingdom of heaven is included under the kingdom of God and sometimes has the same reference. This means that we should devote a little time to these usages in order to sort them out. There are other kingdoms under the kingdom of God, too; so to be thorough, we need to establish a solid foundational awareness and iron out wrinkles in our understanding and biblical terminology.

A very good friend of mine, Ken Petersen, noticed the difference between the usages of kingdom of God and kingdom of heaven while teaching a group of college students one day. He announced to his class, "I'm not exactly sure what the difference is, but I'll study it tonight and tell you tomorrow." Ken did not discover the answer in one night's study, but the trek started him on a quest that led him into deeper commitment and continues to be a rich source of inspiration for him to this day.

The Kingdom of God

In a simple statement, the kingdom of God is in effect from the very beginning all the way throughout eternity. It started with the first heavens and earth, includes the second heavens and earth that are now, and also includes the third heavens and earth that are future. It includes the period of the kingdom of heaven. The kingdom of heaven is the personal presence of the King from heaven on the earth. Anytime the King is present on the earth, the kingdom of heaven is in effect.

As simple as that statement may be, since we are dealing with different kingdoms and different inheritances, it is necessary to explore this subject even deeper. There is an inheritance for the kingdom of heaven which is distinct and separate from the others. Outside of the gospel of Matthew, when the inheritance of the kingdom of God is mentioned, it includes the 1,000-year reign of Jesus on the earth.

An explanation of the word "kingdom" will help to simplify matters. It is the Greek word *basileia* and simply means "the reign of a king." There are many separate and distinct kingdoms underneath the overall heading of the kingdom of God. There is the reign of King David and all other kings on the earth, inclusive of bad kings like Nimrod and Ahab. There is a kingdom of priests where select groups of people reign as the representatives of the true King of heaven.

A major point of explanation is needed here. There are different sub-sections of time beneath the all-inclusive, overall kingdom of God. One includes Father Yahweh as the Supreme Potentate; during another period of time the Holy Spirit will oversee affairs; yet another involves Jesus Christ sitting upon His throne and ruling. Ignorance of this has made it difficult to separate the different kingdoms and to clearly define the inheritances within each kingdom.

I will give examples of these, but first an additional word of explanation will clear up this matter quite well and also give clarity to the subject of the Trinity. This deals with the proper name of our Father God, Yahweh.[1] When the New Testament was translated into Greek, the name of *Yahweh* was considered so sacred that no one wanted to write it. So, instead of transliterating the proper name of our Father Yahweh, they simply translated His name as "God." This caused great confusion because, as we all know, there are many gods (Psalm 82:6; John 10:30). However, we know that when it comes to being Almighty God, there is really only one—our Father Yahweh.

Appendix B

> *For though there be that are called gods, whether in heaven or in earth, (as there be gods many, and lords many,) But to us there is but one God, the Father, of whom are all things, and we in him; and one Lord Jesus Christ, by whom are all things, and we by him.*
> *1 Corinthians 8:5–6*

This mistranslation of our Father's proper name has caused incredible confusion.[2] No one should ever question that Jesus is God or that the Holy Spirit is God, but because of this improper translation of *Yahweh* into the Greek (and now into the English), we not only have the persons of the Trinity being confused, but their respective kingdoms as well. So when we use the phrase "kingdom of God" we have no accurate basis for distinguishing which kingdom we are referring to, except the context of the passage and the scope of the scripture relating to the usage.

For example, there is no doubt that the Father has a kingdom. Perhaps the most clear scripture that shows the difference between the kingdom of the Father and that of the Son is 1 Corinthians 15:24.

> *Then cometh the end [of the millennial kingdom or the kingdom of the Son or the kingdom of heaven], when he [Jesus] shall have delivered up the kingdom to God, even the Father; when he shall have put down all rule and all authority and power.*
> *1 Corinthians 15:24*

This shows that the Father's kingdom is at the end of the millennial kingdom. The Father's kingdom is the new heavens and earth. The following verses document this as well.

> *Then [after the millennial kingdom and the Outer Darkness] shall the righteous shine forth*

> *as the sun in the kingdom of their Father. Who hath ears to hear, let him hear.*
> *Matthew 13:43*
>
> *He that overcometh shall inherit all things [in the new heavens and earth]; and I will be his God, and he shall be my son.   Revelation 21:7*

Likewise, there are many usages of the kingdom of the Son, Jesus Christ. This is the millennial age or the 1,000-year reign of Jesus on the earth.

> *I charge thee therefore before God, and the Lord Jesus Christ, who shall judge the quick and the dead at his appearing and his kingdom.   2 Timothy 4:1*
>
> *For so an entrance shall be ministered unto you abundantly into the everlasting kingdom of our Lord and Saviour Jesus Christ.*
> *2 Peter 1:11*

The kingdom of the Holy Spirit is the age in which we are living now. This is the mystery era between the suffering and glory of the Lord. Jesus sent the Holy Spirit as the personal liaison of the Godhead to the earth to have His reign over the earth during this time period. When the apostles asked Jesus if He was going to restore the kingdom to Israel, Jesus told them about this mystery era.

> *When they therefore were come together, they asked of him, saying, Lord, wilt thou at this time restore again the kingdom to Israel? And he said unto them, It is not for you to know the times or the seasons, which the Father hath put in his own power. But ye shall receive power, after that the Holy Ghost is come upon you: and ye shall be witnesses unto me both in*

Appendix B

> *Jerusalem, and in all Judaea, and in Samaria, and unto the uttermost part of the earth.*
> *Acts 1:6–8*

This era is referred to as the last days of the week of millennia.

> *And it shall come to pass in the last days, saith God, I will pour out of my Spirit upon all flesh: and your sons and your daughters shall prophesy, and your young men shall see visions, and your old men shall dream dreams: And on my servants and on my handmaidens I will pour out in those days of my Spirit; and they shall prophesy.*
> *Acts 2:17–18*

Once we begin to see the distinctions between these kingdoms and their rulers, it becomes clearer to our understanding which one is being referenced as we read through Scripture. For example, Mark 9:1 is a verse that has puzzled Bible teachers and scholars for years. By the context, however, we can now determine that this refers to the kingdom of the Holy Spirit, which those witnessing the words of Jesus saw before their death.

> *And he said unto them, Verily I say unto you, That there be some of them that stand here, which shall not taste of death, till they have seen the kingdom of God come with power.*
> *Mark 9:1*

We also need to remember that the kingdom of God is already in existence on the earth now and is not reserved for the future only. The kingdom of God is being built now, but the kingdom of heaven is held in abeyance until the return of the King from heaven.

The Kingdom of Heaven

Usages of the kingdom of heaven are reserved only for the gospel of Matthew, where it occurs 31 times. The reason it is only used here is that Matthew's report deals with Jesus as King.[3] Many of the details and specifics we know about the coming kingdom here on earth come from Matthew.

In an interesting side note, each of the four gospels portrays Jesus in different aspects: Matthew as King; Mark as a servant; Luke as the Son of Man, and John as the Son of God. Matthew gives the lineage of Jesus through David, the king (1:6). It also has the wise men coming and asking where is He that is born King of the Jews (2:2). Hence, we can conclude that Matthew and its usages of the kingdom of heaven refer to the reign of the King on the earth at that time and that the parables of the kingdom of heaven reveal truths about that kingdom, what would happen to it, and the keys to entering it. (See chapter 13, "Keys to Entering the Kingdom.")

Simply stated, the kingdom of heaven involves the personal presence of the King from heaven. It refers both to when Jesus was here before and when He will be on the earth again. It includes the first three-and-a-half years of His first coming and will also be in extant during the 1,000-year reign coming in the future. It involves the sufferings of the Lord and the glory, too.

For example, when John the Baptist said, "Repent, the kingdom of heaven is at hand," he meant that Jesus was on the earth (Matthew 3:2 NKJ). Jesus was referring to the same in Matthew 4:17. This pertained to the first coming of Jesus to the earth.

When Jesus said, "Blessed are the poor in spirit: for theirs is the kingdom of heaven," He was referring to the future rewards for being a disciple (Matthew 5:3). Similarly, in all of the promises in the Beatitudes, these are rewards

Appendix B

reserved in the future reign on the earth for those who serve faithfully now.

> *Blessed are they which are persecuted for righteousness' sake: for theirs is the kingdom of heaven.*   *Matthew 5:10*

Usages of the kingdom of heaven provide many details about the coming reign of Jesus on the earth. There will be degrees of rewards in the kingdom of heaven yet to come on the earth. It will be according to the degree of service you perform.

> *Whosoever therefore shall break one of these least commandments, and shall teach men so, he shall be called the least in the kingdom of heaven: but whosoever shall do and teach them, the same shall be called great in the kingdom of heaven.*   *Matthew 5:19*

> *For unto every one that hath shall be given, and he shall have abundance: but from him that hath not shall be taken away even that which he hath.*   *Matthew 25:29*

All of the usages of the Outer Darkness (see chapter 15) occur in the gospel of Matthew because this depicts the separation from the King and being outside of the kingdom of heaven on earth. Even though the usages of the kingdom of heaven are only found in Matthew, we must remember that the kingdom of God also can refer to the reign of Jesus on the earth. This will clear up a cloudy issue that desperately needs further explanation.

> *Now the works of the flesh are manifest, which are these; Adultery, fornication, uncleanness, lasciviousness, Idolatry, witchcraft, hatred, variance, emulations, wrath, strife, seditions, heresies, Envyings, murders, drunkenness, revellings, and such like: of the which I tell you*

> *before, as I have also told you in time past, that they which do such things shall not inherit the kingdom of God.*
> *Galatians 5:19–21*

This verse has confused many people because of the issue of grace. The belief is that because someone is born again, they have legal rights into the kingdom of God, regardless of what they do. That is true if the reference is being made about the kingdom of the Father—the new heavens and earth, because that is given on the basis of grace, not works. But when the kingdom of God is referring to the kingdom of heaven, or the reign of Jesus on earth, entrance is not guaranteed if the person does not merit the reward according to service and work.

In the case of Galatians 5:19–21, the kingdom of God is referring to the era of the reign of Jesus on earth. We know that if a person practices the works of the flesh, they will not inherit the millennial reign of Jesus on the earth. They may still have grace and eternal life in the new heavens and earth—that is the inheritance of grace, but the inheritance of reward will be given to the good and faithful servant.

It is becoming more evident why knowledge about the usages of the kingdom of God and the kingdom of heaven is needful. By applying that knowledge, we are able to understand usages where the kingdom of God refers to the kingdom of the Father, usages where the kingdom of God refers to the kingdom of the Son, and still others where the kingdom of God refers to the kingdom of the Holy Spirit.

APPENDIX C
CAN YOU LOSE YOUR SALVATION?

One of the most hotly contested questions in the body of Christ is, "Can you lose your salvation?" Obviously, no one wants to get to heaven and find out he or she cannot get in. The volatility of this issue has caused great division among Christian groups. A pastor once seriously scolded me because I taught that Christians have eternal life. Hopefully, between this appendix and appendix F, "The Word 'Eternal,'" this topic can become clearer.

"Saved" is the Greek word *sozo* (Strong's Concordance #4982), and it means "to rescue or keep safe or to deliver from destruction." Once we understand that there are three separate parts of mankind—spirit, soul, and body—it will become easier to see that each of these have different criteria for being saved.

Your spirit is saved by the grace of God; it is a gift. It was given by grace and cannot be lost. This salvation gives you the inheritance of grace and rights into the Father's kingdom or the new heavens and earth. Ephesians 2:8 and Titus 3:4–7 give clear evidence of this salvation. You cannot lose the salvation of the spirit.

> *But after that the kindness and love of God our Saviour toward man appeared, Not by works of righteousness which we have done, but according to his mercy he saved [past tense] us, by the washing of regeneration, and renewing of the Holy Ghost; Which he shed on us abundantly through Jesus Christ our Saviour; That being justified by his grace, we should be made heirs according to the hope of eternal life.*   Titus 3:4–7

Your soul is presently being saved by obedience to the Word of God. When evangelists or well-meaning teachers talk about getting a specific number of souls saved, they are in textual error. The spirit of man is saved by confessing Jesus as Lord; the soul is saved by obedience to the Word of God on a continuing basis.

> *Wherefore lay apart all filthiness and superfluity of naughtiness, and receive with meekness the engrafted word, which is able to save your souls.*   James 1:21

This is of keen interest when dealing with the millennial kingdom. The salvation of the soul certainly can be lost if the person backslides out of faithfulness. I have heard well-meaning ministers stand up and shout to the roof top that you cannot lose your salvation; on the other hand, I have heard equally zealous ministers shout that you can. May I humbly suggest to both of them to consider the following: You are both right, but neither one of you is totally right. I once had a minister tell me he would eat his Bible if I could show him where it said that you could lose your salvation. I handed him 1 Corinthians 15:2, a knife and fork and some salt and pepper.

Appendix C

> *By which also ye are saved, if ye keep in memory what I preached unto you, unless ye have believed in vain.*   1 Corinthians 15:2

I am certain that a Christian cannot lose the salvation of his spirit, but the minister choking on the Bible did not know that there is a salvation of the soul that *can* be lost. Second John 8 says that we are to labor to receive the full rewards coming to us. If anyone wants to receive the fullness of rewards in the millennial kingdom, they must stand faithful to the death so they will receive the crown of life (Revelation 2:10). There is an amazing amount of documentation on this subject throughout the Word of God. You can most definitely lose the salvation of your soul—that is called backsliding!

Concerning the salvation of your body, you have never had it, so to ask if you can lose it is ludicrous. Romans 8:24 says that we are saved by (in) hope. Verse 23 shows exactly the point of the coming salvation of the body, which is future.

> *And not only they, but ourselves also, which have the firstfruits of the Spirit, even we ourselves groan within ourselves, waiting for the adoption, to wit, the redemption of our body. For we are saved by hope: but hope that is seen is not hope: for what a man seeth, why doth he yet hope for?*   Romans 8:23–24

We are waiting for the total redemption of our bodies which will happen at the resurrection. So, we are saved in hope that it will come, and we should patiently wait for it.

One way of looking at salvation is by utilizing the three verbal tenses: past, present, and future. If you are a born-again Christian, your spirit *has been* saved; your soul *is being* saved and your body *will be* saved.

Now we can rightly divide the word of truth in Revelation 3:5 concerning a person's name being blotted out of the book of life.

> *He that overcometh, the same shall be clothed in white raiment; and I will not blot out his name out of the book of life, but I will confess his name before my Father, and before his angels.*   Revelation 3:5

In chapter 7, "The Bride Comes Out of the Body," we covered the usage of white garments. This is what the bride will wear at the marriage supper of the Lamb. So, if you overcome, you will wear white, and your name will not be blotted out of the Lamb's book of life. The Lamb has a book, and the Father has a book (Revelation 20:15). Those who are written in the Father's book will not be blotted out because that deals with the inheritance of grace, but for those who slack off and turn back once they have put their hand to the plow (Luke 9:62), the salvation of their soul and the right to the millennial kingdom is at stake.

May we all be humble in our understanding and admit that we may have been right, but not totally right? May we also admit that our brother, with a different point of view, has been right too?

> *Blessed are the peacemakers for they shall be called the sons of God.*   Matthew 5:9 NKJ

APPENDIX D
Life in the Millennial Kingdom

Life in the millennial kingdom is going to be grand. Those who enter it will be able to sit at the feet of Jesus and hear Him expound on the greatness of life and the love of the Father. We will study war no more (Isaiah 2:4) because we shall live with the Prince of Peace (Isaiah 11:1–5).

It was my initial intent when beginning the study and teaching of this field to paint a word picture of this kingdom in order to motivate Christians to lay down their lives to partake of it. As I have pondered this in my mind, and as the Holy Spirit has revealed things to me, I now know that it is too wonderful to describe. However, the Holy Spirit reveals the deep things of God and will show them to you as He has to me.

To help you grasp these truths, I have enclosed the following table. This took many hours of biblical study to put together, but it has been very helpful for me, and hopefully will be for you too. I trust that as you look up these references, the Holy Spirit will build anticipation in you to be a part of this 1,000-year reign of Jesus on the earth.

There is much more information in both the Old and New Testaments about life in the millennial reign. Studying about "the day of the Lord" will reveal some of these, if you desire to further explore the topic.

Activity	Description	Documentation
Government	• Jesus rules from Jerusalem (Zion)	Psalm 1:2, 48:2, 12–13, 87:3; Isaiah 52:1, 60:18
	• Will not oppress the poor	Psalm 72; Isaiah 11:4
	• Rules with a rod of iron	Psalm 2:9; Revelation 2:26
	• Will study war no more	Isaiah 2:4; Psalm 46:9, 68:30; Micah 4:3
	• Jesus will be the Prince of Peace	Isaiah 9:6, 32:1
	• Jesus will be the King of the World	Isaiah 2:2–3; Psalm 68:29; Matthew 25:32–46
	• David will be king of the Jews	Ezekiel 34:23, 37:24
	• The 12 apostles will rule over the 12 tribes	Matthew 19:28
	• There will be rulers of cities	Luke 19:17–19
	• Jesus will reign with His bride	Hosea 2:16–18; Revelation 19:7–9
Worship	• New temple	Zechariah 6:12–13
	• Shekinah glory will fill the temple	Ezekiel 11:22–23, 43:4–7
	• Gentiles will be allowed in the temple	Isaiah 56:1–8
	• Will keep the Jewish feast days	Jeremiah 17:26; Ezekiel 47:9–11; Zechariah 14:14
	• All idolatry will be abolished	Isaiah 2:12–21
Environment	• Lion will lie down with the lamb	Isaiah 11:6ff
	• No curse on land (no starvation; plenty of food)	Psalm 65:9–13; Joel 3:17–19; Isaiah 35:1–2; Amos 9:13
	• River from throne makes the Dead Sea sweet	Ezekiel 47:1–12; Zechariah 9:10; Joel 3:18
	• Health and longevity for 1,000 years	Isaiah 35:5–6, 10

APPENDIX E
Rewards in the Kingdom of the Father

There is actually triple indemnity for those Christians who faithfully serve the Lord. There are blessings in the reign of the Holy Spirit now; there will be blessings in the millennial kingdom of our Lord Jesus, and there will also be rewards given in the kingdom of the Father.

Throughout our study, we have seen the inheritance of grace and the inheritance of merit and reward given to those who are good and faithful. But God the Father also reserves the right to reward those whom He chooses.

Everyone within the kingdom of the Father receives the inheritance of eternal life in the new heavens and earth—all Christians are heirs of God without respect of persons. God the Father will give every one of His children life in His kingdom, but there is also a reward that will be given to faithful sons, allowing them entrance into the new Jerusalem and the temple of God.

Now, we are talking about the new heavens and earth, not the millennial reign. The things we are looking at now will occur after the great white throne judgment, after death and hell are cast into the lake of fire, after the second heavens and earth have been destroyed, and after all the children of God have been raised from the dead. After all these events have transpired, God the Father will still have special rewards for certain of His children. He is no respecter of persons, but He is a just God, and a rewarder of those who diligently seek Him.

> *And I saw a new heaven and a new earth: for the first heaven and the first earth were passed away; and there was no more sea. And I John saw the holy city, new Jerusalem, coming down from God out of heaven, prepared as a bride adorned for her husband.*
> *Revelation 21:1–2*

The new Jerusalem will be given as a gift to the bride of Christ. It goes on to say in Revelation 21 that God will wipe away all tears and sorrows and His sons will be with Him forever. Then it emphatically says that the second death is over.

> *But the fearful, and unbelieving, and the abominable, and murderers, and whoremongers, and sorcerers, and idolaters, and all liars, shall have their part in the lake which burneth with fire and brimstone: which is the second death.*   *Revelation 21:8*

Then the angel of the Lord took John and showed him the wedding gift for the bride.

> *And there came unto me one of the seven angels which had the seven vials full of the seven last plagues, and talked with me, saying, Come hither, I will shew thee the bride, the Lamb's wife. And he carried me away in the spirit to a great and high mountain, and shewed me that great city, the holy Jerusalem, descending out of heaven from God.*
> *Revelation 21:9–10*

Appendix E

The description of the new Jerusalem continues.

> *And I saw no temple therein: for the Lord God Almighty and the Lamb are the temple of it. And the city had no need of the sun, neither of the moon, to shine in it: for the glory of God did lighten it, and the Lamb is the light thereof. And the nations of them which are saved shall walk in the light of it: and the kings of the earth do bring their glory and honour into it.*   Revelation 21:22–24

Notice who gets to go into the new Jerusalem.

> *And there shall in no wise enter into it any thing that defileth, neither whatsoever worketh abomination, or maketh a lie: but they which are written in the Lamb's book of life.*   Revelation 21:27

When I first saw this truth I tried to disprove it, but there were other related verses that said the same thing.

> *Blessed are they that do his commandments, that they may have right to the tree of life, and may enter in through the gates into the city. For without are dogs, and sorcerers, and whoremongers, and murderers, and idolaters, and whosoever loveth and maketh a lie.*
>   Revelation 22:14–15

There are other scriptures that tell us the same truth—that those who do not make the millennial kingdom, namely those whose names are not written in the Lamb's book of life, will not have rewards in the kingdom of the Father. Ephesians 5 says it about the kingdom of Christ and of God the Father.

> *For this ye know, that no whoremonger, nor unclean person, nor covetous man, who is an*

> *idolater, hath any inheritance in the kingdom of Christ and of God.*   Ephesians 5:5

This bothered me for quite some time when I realized that it appears there is still a residual effect to those who did not make the millennial kingdom in the kingdom of the Father. Then I realized this is not a punishment to those who did not make the millennial kingdom of the Lord, but a wedding gift, or reward, to the bride for her faithful service with the Lord during the millennial reign.

This sweetens the pot even more than before. We are competing against the devil and our flesh to show ourselves worthy to reign with the Lord in His kingdom and also to qualify for honor from God the Father for our faithful service.

Thank God for His grace and mercy—that He will allow all believers to live with Him in the new heavens and earth forever and for the beautiful gift of the new Jerusalem to the bridegroom and bride for their faithful service during the millennial kingdom.

APPENDIX F
The Word "Eternal"

The word "eternal" warrants a deeper understanding as it is used in the King James Version and other English versions of the Bible. It is the Greek word *aionios* as an adjective and *aion* as a noun. Since the millennial kingdom is referred to as having an end and these two words are loosely translated either "eternal" or "everlasting," we need to closely examine their usages.[a]

According to the Vine's Expository Dictionary, *aion* means "an age." When the age referred to is the new heavens and earth, which has no end, a translation as "eternal" makes sense. But when the age being referenced is not the new heavens and earth, then a rendering as "eternal" is not accurate.

There are a number of ages in the Bible as we discussed in chapter 3, "The Outline of the Ages." The final one will truly be eternal, but all others have definite time limitations. So, when we read verses about the millennial kingdom being an eternal reign, it can be confusing. The prominent verse that can be hard to understand is 2 Peter 1:11.

> *For so an entrance shall be ministered unto you abundantly into the everlasting [aionios] kingdom of our Lord and Saviour Jesus Christ.*
> 2 Peter 1:11

What this says is that an entrance will be granted to you in the kingdom of the age of the Lord and Savior Jesus Christ. That age will last 1,000 years and will not be eternal in the literal sense.

On the other hand, when *aion* is used concerning the age of the kingdom of the Father, it truly *is* eternal, meaning that it will be everlasting and go on forever and ever and ever.

> *For God so loved the world, that he gave his only begotten Son, that whosoever believeth in him should not perish, but have everlasting [aionios] life.*
> John 3:16

With this understanding many unclear verses can now be understood.

For your reference, the following table is a complete listing of every usage of *aion* and *aionion* in the singular and plural occurrences for the New Testament.

Occurrences of Aion & Aionion in Greek New Testament

Singular	Singular	Singular
Matthew 12:32	John 4:14	Romans 6:22
Matthew 13:22	John 4:36	Romans 6:23
Matthew 13:39	John 5:24	Romans 12:2
Matthew 13:40	John 5:39	Romans 16:26
Matthew 13:49	John 6:27	1 Corinthians 1:20
Matthew 18:8	John 6:40	1 Corinthians 2:6 (2x)
Matthew 19:16	John 6:47	1 Corinthians 2:8
Matthew 19:29	John 6:51	1 Corinthians 3:18
Matthew 21:19	John 6:54	1 Corinthians 8:13
Matthew 24:3	John 6:58	2 Corinthians 4:4
Matthew 25:41	John 6:68	2 Corinthians 4:17
Matthew 25:46	John 8:35 (2x)	2 Corinthians 5:1
Matthew 28:20	John 8:51	2 Corinthians 9:9
Mark 3:29 (2x)	John 8:52	Galatians 1:4
Mark 4:19	John 9:32	Galatians 6:8
Mark 10:17	John 10:28	Ephesians 1:21
Mark 10:30 (2x)	John 11:26	Ephesians 2:2
Mark 11:14	John 12:25	Ephesians 6:12
Luke 1:55	John 12:34	2 Thessalonians 1:9
Luke 1:70	John 12:50	2 Thessalonians 2:16
Luke 10:25	John 13:8	1 Timothy 1:16
Luke 16:8	John 14:16	1 Timothy 6:12
Luke 18:18	John 17:2	1 Timothy 6:16
Luke 18:30 (2x)	John 17:3	1 Timothy 6:17
Luke 20:34	Acts 3:21	1 Timothy 6:19
Luke 20:35	Acts 13:46	2 Timothy 2:10
John 3:15	Acts 13:48	2 Timothy 4:10
John 3:16	Acts 15:18	Titus 1:2
John 3:36	Romans 5:21	Titus 2:12

Singular

Titus 3:7
Philemon 1:15
Hebrews 1:8 (2x)
Hebrews 5:6
Hebrews 5:9
Hebrews 6:2
Hebrews 6:5
Hebrews 6:20
Hebrews 7:17
Hebrews 7:21
Hebrews 7:24
Hebrews 7:28
Hebrews 9:12
Hebrews 9:14
Hebrews 9:15
Hebrews 13:20
1 Peter 1:23
1 Peter 1:25
1 Peter 5:10
2 Peter 1:11
2 Peter 2:17
2 Peter 3:18
1 John 1:2
1 John 2:17
1 John 2:25
1 John 3:15
1 John 5:11
1 John 5:13
1 John 5:20

Singular

2 John 2
Jude 1:7
Jude 1:13
Jude 1:21
Revelation 14:6

Plural

Matthew 6:13
Luke 1:33
Luke 16:9
Romans 1:25
Romans 9:5
Romans 11:36
Romans 16:25
Romans 16:27
1 Corinthians 2:7
1 Corinthians 10:11
2 Corinthians 4:18
2 Corinthians 11:31
Galatians 1:5 (2x)
Ephesians 2:7
Ephesians 3:9
Ephesians 3:11
Philippians 4:20 (2x)
Colossians 1:26
1 Timothy 1:17 (3x)
2 Timothy 1:9

Plural

2 Timothy 4:18 (2x)
Hebrews 1:2
Hebrews 9:26
Hebrews 11:3
Hebrews 13:8
Hebrews 13:21 (2x)
1 Peter 4:11 (2x)
1 Peter 5:11 (2x)
Jude 1:25
Revelation 1:6 (2x)
Revelation 1:18 (2x)
Revelation 4:9 (2x)
Revelation 4:10 (2x)
Revelation 5:13 (2x)
Revelation 5:14 (2x)
Revelation 7:12 (2x)
Revelation 10:6 (2x)
Revelation 11:15 (2x)
Revelation 14:11 (2x)
Revelation 15:7 (2x)
Revelation 19:3 (2x)
Revelation 20:10 (2x)
Revelation 22:5 (2x)

Singular & Plural

Ephesians 3:21 (2x)

APPENDIX G
MATTHEW 24:14

Matthew 24:14 has been a thorn in the side of many eschatologists. They have had great difficulty explaining it because they do not differentiate between the gospel of grace and the gospel of the kingdom.

> *And this gospel of the kingdom shall be preached in all the world for a witness unto all nations; and then shall the end come.*
> *Matthew 24:14*

Not recognizing the difference between the gospel of the kingdom and the gospel of grace has led Bible teachers to propound that the gospel (of grace or salvation of the spirit) must be preached in all the world before the Lord can return. NO! The verse says the gospel of the kingdom, so those who have used this verse as a cornerstone of doctrine for "rapture theory" have built a crooked house.

Some may think that if this is the case, we will never see the end times or the return of the Lord. They say, "We are having a hard enough time getting the gospel of grace around the world, so does this mean that we must now witness the gospel of the kingdom before the end will come?" The explanation of how this will happen is very simple and yet it reveals another aspect of the gospel of the kingdom.

The 1,000 Year Reign of Jesus Christ on the Earth

The gospel of the kingdom, or the good news of the 1,000-year reign of Jesus on the earth, absolutely will be preached in all the world for a witness before the end will come, but it will be done by angels and not men. This will occur during the great tribulation that Jesus was referring to in Matthew 24:14. Between the second and third woes during the great tribulation, trials and torments will become so great that many of the elect will be deceived into taking the mark of the beast. This will be a crucial period during the counterfeit rule of the antichrist who will deceive the world into thinking that he is the real Christ. At that time, an angel will fly throughout the world and strengthen the saints by reminding them that there is a kingdom coming, and if they do not take the mark of the beast, they can be part of it. This happens just prior to the great harvest at the end of the world.

> *And I saw another angel fly in the midst of heaven, having the everlasting gospel to preach unto them that dwell on the earth, and to every nation, and kindred, and tongue, and people.*   Revelation 14:6

The angel will witness of the gospel of the kingdom and tell people to hold on just a little longer so that they will be "reaped" at the end of the world and will be granted rights into Jesus' 1,000-year reign. Notice that in Revelation 14:7–11 the angels say to worship only God and not to take the mark of the beast. This is a direct reference to the Lord's requirements for entering the kingdom of Christ on the earth.

> *And I saw thrones, and they sat upon them, and judgment was given unto them: and I saw the souls of them that were beheaded for the witness of Jesus, and for the word of God, and which had not worshipped the beast, neither his image, neither had received his mark upon*

Appendix G

> *their foreheads, or in their hands; and they lived and reigned with Christ a thousand years.*   *Revelation 20:4*

The witness of the angel testifying of the coming of the kingdom between the second and third woes will give the saints patience and strength to stand to the end and not take the mark of the beast. Those who remain faithful till the end will be saved (Matthew 24:13). The witness by the angel about the coming kingdom will give them the faith to stand on the commandment of God (and if necessary to die in the Lord) in order to make the millennial kingdom.

> *Here is the patience of the saints: here are they that keep the commandments of God, and the faith of Jesus. And I heard a voice from heaven saying unto me, Write, Blessed are the dead which die in the Lord from henceforth: Yea, saith the Spirit, that they may rest [in the kingdom] from their labours; and their works do follow them [into the millennial kingdom].*
>   *Revelation 14:12–13*

NOTES

Chapter 1
The Two Gospels

1. Romans 1:1, 15:16; 2 Corinthians 11:7; 1 Thessalonians 2:2, 8–9; and 1 Peter 4:17.

2. Romans 1:16, 15:19 and 29; 1 Corinthians 9:12, 18; 2 Corinthians 4:4, 9:13, 10:14; Galatians 1:7; Philippians 1:27; and 1 Thessalonians 3:2.

Chapter 2
The Kingdom Lost

1. James H. Rutz, *The Open Church* (Auburn, ME: Seedsowers, 1992), 8.

2. Matthew 10:39, 16:25, 19:29; Mark 8:35; Luke 9:24. Second Corinthians 4:8–14 also shows this truth and offers the reward of inheritance as the factor to strengthen us in times of persecution.

3. Paul McKechnie, *The First Christian Centuries* (Downers Grove, IL: InterVarsity Press, 2001), 234–236.

4. *Jesus and His Times* (Pleasantville, NY: Reader's Digest Association, 1987), 303. Constantine refused Christian

baptism until the day of his death, on Pentecost Sunday, May 22, 337.

5. Grant R. Jeffrey, *Heaven, The Mystery of Angels* (Toronto, Canada: Frontier Research Publications, 1996), 47–48.

Chapter 3
The Outline of the Ages

1. This belief is hinged upon the first usage of "was" in Genesis 1:2, which could be translated "became." The following verses (2–10) show the restructuring of the flooded cosmos. This means that the original heavens and earth were destroyed and the one in which we live now (the second) is the one God revamped.

2. The verb is middle deponent and is translated "became," or by the action of Holy Spirit, John "was taken" into the spirit realm to observe the things to take place in the seventh day of the week of millennia.

Chapter 5
The Sufferings and the Glory of the Lord

1. E.W. Bullinger, *Witness of the Stars* (1893, Reprint 1975, Grand Rapids, MI: Kregel Publications), 23–26.

Chapter 7
The Bride Comes Out of the Body

1. E.W. Bullinger, *Witness of the Stars* (1893, Reprint 1975. Grand Rapids, MI: Kregel Publications), 103–104 and 107–112.

Chapter 12
Laboring to Enter into the Rest

1. Andrew Murray, *The Holiest of All* (Springdale, PA: Whitaker House, 1996), 151.

Chapter 15
The Outer Darkness

1. Dale M. Sides, "The Outer Darkness," Episkopos Tape EP16; Bedford, VA: Liberating Ministries for Christ International (LMCI), 1997.

Chapter 16
Gehenna

1. Dale M. Sides, "Have Salt in Yourself and Peace with One Another," Episkopos Tape EP31; Bedford, VA: LMCI, 2001.

Appendix A
The Woman Who Hid the Kingdom

1. Ralph Woodrow, *Babylon Mystery Religion* (Riverside, CA: Ralph Woodrow Evangelistic Association, 1966), 13.

2. *Zondervan Encyclopedia of the Bible* (Grand Rapids, MI: Zondervan Publishing, 1975), Volume 4, 712.

3. Woodrow, *Babylon Mystery Religion*, 14.

4. Ibid., 14.

5. Lorainne Boettner, "Roman Catholicism," (Philadelphia, PA: Philadelphia Presbyterian and Reformed Publishing Co., 1989), 147.

Appendix B
The Kingdom of God and the Kingdom of Heaven

1. Vicki Sides, *Yahweh—The Sacred Name of God*, audiocassette tape set TA16, available through LMCI.

2. Dale M. Sides, "I Believe in the Godhead, but I'm Not So Sure about the Trinity," LMCI. Access online at http://www.lmci.org/articles.cfm?Article=78.

3. E.W. Bullinger, *The Companion Bible*, Appendix 96; "The Diversity of the Four Gospels," (Grand Rapids, MI: Kregel Publications, 1990), 140.

INDEX

Page numbers are italicized. Following a page number, "n" denotes an endnote; "t" denotes a table.

A

Abraham, *31, 68*
Acts
  1:6, *46*
  1:6–8, *178–179*
  1:7–8, *46*
  2:17, *31*
  2:17–18, *179*
  3:21, *195t*
  13:46, *195t*
  13:48, *195t*
  14:22, *116t*
  15:18, *195t*
  17:6–8, *20*
  18:17, *80*
  19:27, *166*
  20:24, *12*
Adam, *30–31, 62, 63–65, 69*
age(s) *7, 26–33*
  church, *157–158, 168*
  harvest, at end of, *129*
  kingdom of the Holy Spirit, *178*
  length of, *193–194*
  of grace, *160*
aggello, *10*
agonizomai, *111–112*
aion, *193–196*
aionion, *194–196*
aionios, *193–194*
amillenarians, *42*
Amos 9:13, *188t*
ana, *87*
anastasis, *87*
antichrist, *38, 84, 196*
Aphrodite, *165, 168*

apo, *90*
apoleia, *90*
apostles (the 12), *49, 133, 188t*
Aramaic text, *125*
athleo, *111*
Augustine, *2, 24, 172*

B

Babylon, *164, 165, 168*
Babylon Mystery Religion, *203n1 (app. A), 203n3, 203n4*
baptism, *76, 101t, 201n4*
basileia, *176*
Baxter, Mary, *137*
Beatitudes, *107, 180–181*
bema, *80–81*
body
  new, *86, 132*
  glorious, glorified, *91, 131–132*
  physical, *91, 109–111, 132, 138*
  salvation of, *185*
  spirit, soul, and, *183–186*
Boettner, Lorainne, *204n5*
bride of Christ, *36, 38, 49, 62–70, 162–164, 173, 188t, 190, 192*
Bride of Christ Wears Combat Boots, The, *68*
Bullinger, E.W. *202n1 (chap. 5), 202n1 (chap. 7), 204n3*

C

Calvary, *10*
Cassiopeia (the Queen constellation), *63*
Cephas (the King constellation), *63*

205

Index

character, 95, 107–108, 162
charis, 13
City of God, The, 24
Colossians
  1:12–13, 13
  1:13, 61t
  1:26, 196t
  3:3, 73
  3:23–24, 54
  3:23–25, 4, 56
  3:24, 58
  3:24–25, 82
  3:25, 82
Companion Bible, The, 204n3
Constantine (emperor of Rome), 2, 22–23, 24, 201n4
1 Corinthians
  1:20, 195t
  2:6, 195t
  2:7, 196t
  2:7–8, 35, 44, 157
  2:8, 195t
  3 (chapter), 82–83
  3:8, 83
  3:10–13, 83
  3:13–15, 138
  3:16–17, 138
  3:18, 195t
  4:1, 10
  8:5–6, 177
  8:13, 195t
  9:12, 18, 201n2 (chap. 1)
  9:17, 109–110
  9:25, 110, 111–112
  9:27, 109–111
  10:11, 196t
  15:2, 184, 185
  15:24, 91, 145, 177
  15:25–26, 145
  15:27–28, 145
  15:32, 21
  15:45–47, 64
2 Corinthians
  4:4, 195t, 201n2 (chap. 1)
  4:8–14, 201n2 (chap. 2)
  4:17, 195t
  4:18, 196t
  5:1, 195t
  5:10, 80, 160

2 Corinthians (continued)
  5:11, 80–81
  5:17, 73
  9:9, 195t
  9:13, 17, 201n2 (chap. 1)
  10:14, 201n2 (chap. 1)
  11:7, 201n1 (chap. 1)
  11:31, 196t
Council of Nicea, 23, 166
crown(s), 84, 111–112, 113–114

D

Daniel (book), 42
Daniel
  2:44, 15, 21, 34, 42, 165
  9:24, 37
Daniel (70th week of), 37–38
day of the Lord, 32, 46–50, 69, 139, 187. *See also* Lord's Day
David (king of Israel), 31, 49, 188t
Deuteronomy 32:51–52, 120
Diana, 166, 168
"Diversity of the Four Gospels, The," 204n3
Divine Revelation of Hell, The, 137

E

ek, 64–65, 87, 127
ekklesia, 66
Eliezer (representing the Holy Spirit), 68
Ephesians (book), 62, 63, 147
Ephesians
  1:10, 129, 146–147
  1:11–14, 147
  1:21, 195t
  2:2, 195t
  2:4, 196t
  2:8, 13, 56, 61t, 183
  3:4–6, 157
  3:5, 44
  3:9, 196t
  3:11, 196t
  3:21, 196t
  5 (chapter), 63, 191
  5:5, 191–192
  5:30, 64, 65
  5:30–32, 64

INDEX

Ephesians *(continued)*
  5:31, 63
  5:32, 64
  5:5, 191–192
  6:12, 172–173, 195t
epistles, Pauline, 16, 17
eternal
  life, 3, 9, 11, 54–56, 141
  word study of, 193–196
eu, 10
euaggellos, 10
exanastasis, 87–88, 113
ex, 87
exo, 127
Exodus 17:6, 119
exoteros, 127
Ezekiel (book), 44
Ezekiel
  11:22–23, 188t
  34:23, 188t
  34:23–24, 49
  37:24, 188t
  37:4–10, 87
  43:4–7, 188t
  47:1–12, 188t
  47:9–11, 188t

F

fear, 94, 95–96, 111, 122, 141
  Him (God), 137–138
  of the Lord, 5, 84, 123
First Christian Centuries, The, 201n3

G

Galatians
  1:4, 195t
  1:5, 196t
  1:7, 201n2 (chap. 1)
  1:8–9, 9
  2:20, 73
  2:21, 106
  5:19–21, 181–182
  6:7, 4
  6:8, 195t
  6:9, 89, 114
gathering together of the church, 36–40, 41, 45. *See also* rapture
Gehenna (*ge'enna*), 133–142, 146, 147, 148–149

Genesis (book), 44, 62
Genesis
  1:1–10, 27
  1:2, 202n1 (chap. 3)
  1:2–10, 202n1 (chap. 3)
  2:21–24, 63–64
  2:23, 64
  2:24, 63–64
  24 (chapter), 68
Gentile(s), 46, 188t
  fullness of, 37, 45
  priesthood, 31–32, 37, 45
gnashing of teeth. *See* teeth, gnashing of
gospel
  of Christ, 16, 17–18
  of grace compared to that of the kingdom, 10–18
  definition of, 10
  of God, 16–17
  of grace, 2, 11, 12, 13–15, 16, 24, 197
  of the kingdom, 2–3, 7, 11, 12, 15–16, 17, 18, 19–25, 161, 167, 197–199
Gospel of the Kingdom, The (class), 122
great mystery. *See under* mystery
great tribulation, 36, 37, 38, 39, 68, 79, 129, 198–199
Gregory XIV (pope), 171
Greek words. *See* listings of individual words

H

hades, 134
"Hail Mary," 171
"Have Salt in Yourself and Peace with One Another," 203n1 (chap. 16)
Heaven, the Mystery of Angels, 24, 202n5
heavens and earth
  end-time sequence and, 34–40
  first (former, original, past), 26–27, 175, 202n1 (chap. 3)
  in the kingdom of God, 175
  new (third, latter, future), 1–2, 14, 16, 28–29, 32, 39, 54, 58, 61t, 73–74, 141–142, 144, 175, 177–178, 183, 189–192, 193–196

INDEX

heavens and earth *(continued)*
  in the outline of the ages, *26–33*
  second (present), *27–30, 31–32, 39, 144–149, 175*
Hebrew words. *See listings of individual words*
Hebrews (book), *99*
Hebrews
  1:2, *31, 196t*
  1:8, *196t*
  2:17, *170*
  3–4 (chapters), *99, 100*
  3:8, 15, *100*
  3:15, *99*
  3:17–19, *99*
  3:19, *100*
  4:1, *100*
  4:7, *100*
  4:9, *32*
  4:9, 11, *100*
  4:9–11, *101–102*
  4:12, *102*
  4:13, *103*
  4:15–16, *171*
  5:6, *196t*
  5:9, *196t*
  5:13, *61t*
  5:14, *61t*
  6:2, *196t*
  6:4, *140*
  6:5, *196t*
  6:8, *141*
  6:9, *141*
  6:10–12, *142*
  6:17–19, *79*
  6:18, *74*
  6:20, *196t*
  7:17, *196t*
  7:21, *196t*
  7:24, *196t*
  7:25–26, *169–170*
  7:28, *196t*
  9:12, *196t*
  9:14, *196t*
  9:15, *196t*
  9:26, *196t*
  11:3, *196t*
  12:6, *132*
  13:8, *196t*

Hebrews *(continued)*
  13:20, *196t*
  13:21, *196t*
heirs of God, *58, 59, 189*
  inheritance of, *53–55*
hell, *129, 133–134, 137–138*
history, church, *20–25, 156, 166*
Holiest of All, The, *102, 203n1 (chap. 12)*
Holy Spirit. *See* Eliezer; kingdom of the
Hosea 2:16–18, *188t*
Hosea 2:16–20, *63, 69*
huios, *59–60*
hymn (song), *73, 152*. *See also* song

I

"I Believe in the Godhead, but I'm Not so Sure about the Trinity," *204n2*
inheritance(s), *51–76*. *See also* inheritance of grace; inheritance of reward
  two kinds of, *16, 53, 56, 58–59, 60, 61t*
inheritance of grace, *14–15, 54–56, 61t, 71, 73–74, 183, 186*
  of being a child, *59–60, 61t*
  eternal life, *54, 108, 189*
  Father's kingdom, *54–56, 59–60, 61t*
inheritance of reward. *See also* reward(s) of (the) inheritance
  of being a son, *59–60, 61t*
  kingdom of heaven, *56, 176*
  of merit, *15, 189*
  millennial kingdom (1,000-year reign), *21, 61t*
  new heavens and earth, *16, 39, 61t, 75, 151, 189*
  of obedience, *61t*
  of service, *75*
  Son's kingdom, *54, 56–58, 59–60, 61t*
  2 Timothy 2:11–13 and, *71, 73, 74*
Isaac, *67–68*
Isaiah (book), *42, 44*
Isaiah
  2: 2–3, *188t*
  2:4, *3, 187, 188t*

INDEX

Isaiah *(continued)*
  2:12–21, *188t*
  9:6, *188t*
  9:6–7, *42–43*
  10:16–17, *139*
  10:18, *139–140*
  11:1–5, *48, 187*
  11:4, *188t*
  11:6, *188t*
  24:23, *172*
  32:1, *188t*
  35:1–2, *188t*
  35:5–6, *188t*
  35:5–6, 10, *188t*
  40:5, *41*
  52:1, *188t*
  56:1–8, *188t*
  60:18, *188t*
Israel. *See also* Jews
  bride of Christ and, *68*
  David reigning over, *49, 188t*
  end-time sequence and, *36, 37, 38, 39*
  great mystery era and, *44–46*
  rejecting Jesus, *41*
  parable of wedding banquet and, *65–66*
  parables spoken to, *157*
  Promised Land journey being a parallel of the millennial reign, *99–104*
  12 tribes of, *49, 188t*

J

Jacob's Trouble, *37*
James
  1:12, *84*
  1:21, *61t, 184*
  2:17, *74*
  3:6, *134, 141*
Jeffrey, Grant, *24, 202n5*
Jeremiah (book), *44*
Jeremiah
  7:17–18, *164*
  7:18, *162, 164*
  7:31–33, *134*
  17:26, *188t*
  30:7, *37*
  44:17–19, 25, *162, 164*

Jeremiah *(continued)*
  44:19, *164, 167*
Jerusalem, new, *189–192*
Jesus and His Times, *201n4*
Jews (Jewish) *34, 38, 157, 188t. See also* Israel
Job (book), *49*
Job
  19:25, *50*
Joel
  3:17–19, *188t*
  3:18, *188t*
John (book), *180*
John
  3:3, *13*
  3:3, 5 *119, 120–121*
  3:5–6, *116t*
  3:15, *195t*
  3:16, *55, 61t, 194, 195t*
  3:36, *195t*
  4:14, *195t*
  4:36, *195t*
  5:24, *195t*
  5:39, *195t*
  6:27, *195t*
  6:40, *195t*
  6:47, *195t*
  6:51, *195t*
  6:54, *195t*
  6:58, *195t*
  6:68, *195t*
  8:35, *195t*
  8:51, *195t*
  8:52, *195t*
  9:32, *195t*
  10:28, *195t*
  10:30, *176*
  11:26, *195t*
  12:25, *195t*
  12:34, *195t*
  12:50, *195t*
  13:8, *195t*
  14:16, *195t*
  16:7–8, *109*
  17:2, *195t*
  17:3, *195t*
  21 (chapter), *75*
  21:15–17, *136*
1 John 1:2, *196t*

INDEX

1 John *(continued)*
   2:17, *196t*
   2:25, *196t*
   3:15, *196t*
   5:11, *196t*
   5:13, *196t*
   5:20, *196t*
2 John (book), *84*
2 John
   2, *196t*
   8, *61t, 85, 185*
3 John 9–10, *135*
John the Baptist, *15, 97, 108–109, 180*
Johnson, Lonnell, *81*
joint-heir(s), *58–59, 113*
Joshua 15:8, *134*
Jude
   1:7, *196t*
   1:13, *140, 196t*
   1:21, *196t*
   1:23, *141*
   1:25, *196t*
judgment. *See also* judgment seat of Christ
   criterion for outer darkness, *126t*
   great white throne, *144, 189*
   Hebrews 4:12–13 and, *102–103*
   queen of heaven trying to hide truth of, *165*
judgment seat of Christ, *79–85, 115*
   end-time events and, *36, 39, 41*
   Gehenna and, *138*
   new body and, *132*
   outer darkness and, *129–130*
   parable of drag net and, *160*

K

kaleo, *66*
kingdom of the Father, *105*
   as distinct from Son's and Holy Spirit's, *177–179*
   as inheritance, *61t*
   Galatians 5:19–21 and, *181–182*
   millennial kingdom's timing and, *144–149*
   rewards in, *189–192*
kingdom of God, *174–179*

kingdom of God *(continued)*
   citizens of, *13*
   referring to other kingdoms, *181–182*
   within you, *14*
kingdom of heaven, *180–182*
   clarification between kingdom of God and, *174–175*
   hiding of it, *155–173*
   as inheritance of reward, *56–59*
   keys from Matthew 5–7, *107–108*
   parable of Matthew 22 and, *65–66*
   parable of Matthew 25:14–30 and, *93–98*
   parables of Matthew 13 summary and, *158–161*
kingdom of the Holy Spirit, *178–179*
kingdom of the Son (Christ): *191–192*
   as distinct from Father's and Holy Spirit's, *177–179*
   inheritance of reward in, *56–61t*
2 Kings 23:10, *134*
koinonos, *113*
Korah, *136–137*

L

lake of fire
   death and hell's fate, *134, 145, 189*
   devil's (Satan's) fate, *19, 39, 144, 145*
last (latter) days, *31–32*
leaven
   identity of woman hiding it, *162–166*
   parable of, *159, 161–162*
   three measures of meal and, *167–169*
Liguori, Alphonsus, *171*
life. *See also* eternal life
   book of, *186, 191*
   in millennial kingdom, *187–188t*
   poem about, *81–82*
   stewardship of physical body in, *109–111*
logon, *81*
Lord's Day, *32. See also* day of the Lord
Luke (book), *180*
Luke
   1:33, *196t*

INDEX

Luke *(continued)*
  1:55, *195t*
  1:70, *195t*
  9:24, *201n2 (chap. 2)*
  9:62, *186*
  10:25, *195t*
  12:1, *162*
  12:32, *4, 89, 116*
  12:4–5, *137*
  12:48, *94*
  13:18–19, *174*
  13:28, *124, 126t*
  16:8, *195t*
  16:9, *196t*
  16:10, *110*
  17:21, *14*
  18:18, *195t*
  18:30, *195t*
  19 (chapter), *93, 95*
  19:17, *73*
  19:17–19, *49, 188t*
  19:22, *97*
  20:34, *195t*
  20:35, *195t*
Luther, Martin, *24, 171*

M

Malachi 4:1, *139*
Mark (book), *180*
Mark
  3:29, *195t*
  4:19, *195t*
  8:15, *162*
  8:35, *201n2 (chap. 2)*
  9:1, *179*
  9:43, *135*
  9:43, 45, 47, *134, 135*
  9:45, *135*
  9:47, *134*
  10:17, *195t*
  10:30, *195t*
  11:14, *195t*
marriage supper of the Lamb
  judgment seat of Christ and, *115*
  many called but few chosen, *75*
  outer darkness and, *130*
  parable of the wedding and, *65–66*
  timing of, *38*
  wedding garment of, *67*

martyrdom, *21–22*
Mary the Mother of God, *166, 168, 169, 170–171*
masteries, striving for, *5, 14, 25, 85, 111–112*
Matthew (book), *61t, 94, 104, 123, 126t, 127, 180, 181*
Matthew
  1:6, *180*
  2:2, *180*
  3:1–2, *12, 15*
  3:2, *61t, 108, 180*
  4:17, *15, 56, 61t, 109, 180*
  4:23, *15*
  5–7 (chapters), *107–108*
  5:3, *180*
  5:9, *186*
  5:10, *181*
  5:19, *181*
  5:20, *108, 116t*
  5:22, *134*
  6:10, *173*
  6:13, *196t*
  7:21–22, *116t*
  7:21–23, *107, 108, 124*
  8:12, *3, 116t, 123, 126t, 127*
  9:35, *12, 15*
  10:24, *75*
  10:39, *201n2 (chap. 2)*
  11 (chapter), *157*
  11:12, *173*
  12:14, *157*
  12:18, *157*
  12:32, *195t*
  13 (chapter), *25, 155–157, 161, 170*
  13:1, *159*
  13:3–9, 18–23, *158*
  13:4, 19, *159*
  13:10–11, *158*
  13:22, *195t*
  13:24–30, 37–43, *158*
  13:28, *18*
  13:31–32, *159, 174–175*
  13:33, *159, 164, 167*
  13:34–35, *157*
  13:39, *195t*
  13:40, *195t*
  13:43, *61t, 177–178*
  13:44, *160*

INDEX

Matthew *(continued)*
  13:45, *160*
  13:47–50, *160*
  13:49, *195t*
  13:52, *160–161*
  16:12, *162*
  16:25, *201n2 (chap. 2)*
  18:3, *116t*
  18:8, *195t*
  19:16, *195t*
  19:23–24, *116t*
  19:28, *49, 188t*
  19:29, *195t, 201n2 (chap. 2)*
  21:19, *195t*
  22 (chapter), *63, 65–66, 67, 160*
  22:7, *66*
  22:9, *66*
  22:12, *116t*
  22:13, *124, 125, 126t, 127*
  22:13–14, *3, 128*
  22:14, *65, 88*
  23:15, *136*
  23:33, *136*
  24:3, *195t*
  24:13, *199*
  24:14, *15, 197–199*
  24:48–51, *136*
  24:51, *124, 126t*
  25 (chapter), *93, 95*
  25:14–15, *94*
  25:14–30, *93*
  25:21, *4, 72, 95, 152*
  25:23, *95*
  25:24–25, *95–96*
  25:24–26, *97*
  25:26–27, *96–97*
  25:26a, 30, *4*
  25:29, *181*
  25:30, *116t, 124, 125, 126t, 127*
  25:32–46, *188t*
  25:41, *195t*
  25:46, *195t*
  26 (chapter), *75*
  28:20, *195t*
McKechnie, Paul, *201n3*
meta, *131*
Micah 4:3, *49, 188t*
Moses, *100, 101t, 119–121, 136, 137*

Murray, Andrew, *102, 203n1 (chap. 12)*
mystery
  era, *31–32, 44–46, 157, 178–179*
  great, *34–37, 44–46*
Mystery Babylon, *162–165, 168–169*

N

Nebuchadnezzar, *164–165*
Numbers
  16:32–33, *137*
  16:35, *137*
  20:8, *119*
  20:12, *120*

O

obedience, *17, 57, 61t, 184–185*
olethropos, *90*
Open Church, The, *20, 201n1 (chap. 2)*
outer darkness, *29, 122–132*
  close of kingdom and, *146–149*
  Matthew 7:21–23 and, *107*
  parable of Matthew 22 and, *65–66*
  parable of Matthew 25:14–30 and, *93–98*
  profile of Moses, *119–121*
"Outer Darkness, The" (audiocassette tape), *203n1 (chap. 15)*

P

parable(s)
  drag net, *160, 173*
  leaven, *159, 161–173*
  Luke 19, *93*
  Matthew 13, *155–173*
  Matthew 22, *65–66*
  Matthew 25, *93–98*
  mustard plant, *159*
  pearl, *160, 173*
  scribe, *160–161*
  sower, *158, 159*
  talents (good and faithful servant), *93–98*
  tares, *158, 159*
  ten virgins (wise and foolish), *93*
  treasure, *160, 173*

INDEX

parable(s) *(continued)*
  wedding banquet, *65–66*
paradise, *129, 130*
Paul (apostle), *21, 113–114*
Pauline epistles, *16, 17*
persecution, *21–23, 25, 74–75, 107, 201n2 (chap. 2)*
Peter, *47, 75*
1 Peter
  1:3–4, *53, 55, 75*
  1:4, *61t*
  1:10–11, *44–45*
  1:17, *4*
  1:23, *196t*
  1:25, *196t*
  4:10, *10*
  4:11, *196t*
  4:13, *49*
  4:17, *16, 201n1 (chap. 1)*
  5:1, *47*
  5:4, *84*
  5:10, *196t*
  5:11, *196t*
2 Peter
  1:4–11, *112–113*
  1:10–11, *116t*
  1:11, *178, 193–194, 196t*
  1:21, *106*
  2:17, *140, 196t*
  3 (chapter), *26–27*
  3:3–4, *27*
  3:5–6, *27*
  3:7, *27–28*
  3:7–10, *29*
  3:8, *30, 131, 132, 139*
  3:10, 12, *29*
  3:13, *14, 28*
  3:15–16, *35, 160*
  3:16, *51*
  3:17, *35*
  3:18, *35–36, 196t*
Petersen, Ken, *175*
Philemon 1:15, *196t*
Philippians
  1:27, *17, 201n2 (chap. 1)*
  3:9–10, *87*
  3:10, *87*
  3:10–21, *86–91*
  3:11, *87–88, 113*

Philippians *(continued)*
  3:12, *88*
  3:13, *88–89*
  3:14, *89*
  3:15, *89*
  3:16, *89*
  3:17, *89–90*
  3:18–19, *90*
  3:20, *90–91*
  3:21, *91, 110, 131*
  4:20, *196t*
Pierce, Elijah, *81*
Pinikir, *165, 168*
Promised Land, *99–101t, 119–121*
Proverbs 14:14, *61*
Psalm
  1:2, *188t*
  2 (chapter), *47*
  2: 6–12, *47*
  2:9, *188t*
  9:17, *134*
  19 (chapter), *63*
  19:1–4, *44*
  24 (chapter), *47*
  24:7–10, *48*
  46:9, *188t*
  47 (chapter), *48*
  47:2–3, *48*
  48:2, 12–13, *188t*
  65:9–13, *188t*
  68:29, *188t*
  68:30, *188t*
  72 (chapter), *188t*
  72:2, *3*
  82:6, *176*
  87:3, *188t*
  90:4, *131*

Q

queen of heaven, *155–173*
  other names for, *165–166*

R

rapture. *See also* gathering together of the church
  of the church, *36–39, 146*
  theory, *197*
Rebekah, *67–69, 106*

reign(ing) with the Lord, *71–76, 78, 84, 91, 146–147*
  Israel's role, *37*
repentance, *46, 56, 61t, 97, 108–109*
resurrection
  definition of, *87*
  of the just, *36, 38*
  out, *86–92, 113–114*
  salvation of body at, *185*
Revelation (book), *38, 49*
Revelation
  1:6, *196t*
  1:10, *32*
  1:18, *196t*
  2–3 (chapters), *17, 56–57*
  2:4, *64*
  2:7, *57*
  2:10, *75, 114, 185*
  2:11, *57*
  2:17, *57*
  2:26, *188t*
  3:5, *57, 186*
  3:12, *57*
  3:19, *132*
  3:21, *58*
  4:1, *37–38*
  4:1–2, *38*
  4:9, *196t*
  4:10, *196t*
  5:10, *43, 72*
  5:13, *128, 196t*
  5:14, *196t*
  7:4, *38*
  7:12, *196t*
  7:14, *37*
  10:6, *196t*
  11:2, *38*
  11:14–18, *83*
  11:15, *72, 196t*
  11:18, *84*
  14 (chapter), *38*
  14:6, *196t, 198*
  14:7–11, *198*
  14:11, *196t*
  14:12–13, *199*
  15–18 (chapters), *38*
  15:7, *196t*
  17:3–5, *163*
  17:5, *163, 165, 168*

Revelation *(continued)*
  18:23, *163*
  19 (chapter), *38*
  19: 3, *196t*
  19:7–8, *38, 163*
  19:7–9, *66, 67, 188t*
  19:11–14, *68*
  19:15, *54*
  19:17–21, *38*
  20:1–3, *3*
  20:1–4, *3*
  20:1–7, *143–144*
  20:4, *21–22, 72, 84, 114, 198–199*
  20:4–5, *38*
  20:6, *2, 72*
  20:7–9, *28, 39*
  20:8–10, *144*
  20:10, *196t*
  20:13–14, *134*
  20:14, *145*
  20:15, *146, 186*
  21 (chapter), *190*
  21–22 (chapters), *29, 54*
  21:1, *14, 29, 144*
  21:1–2, *190*
  21:1–7, *148*
  21:4, *148–149*
  21:7, *3, 54, 178*
  21:8, *190*
  21:9–10, *190*
  21:22–24, *191*
  21:27, *191*
  22:5, *196t*
  22:14–15, *191*
reward(s). *See also* inheritance(s) of reward
  for being a disciple, *180*
  of being His child, *130*
  for character, *95*
  of entering into the joy of the Lord, *95*
  for faithfulness, *95, 180–181, 185*
  for fearing the Lord, *84*
  for finishing the fight, *113–114*
  given to the bride (of Christ), *190*
  of (the) inheritance, *56–58, 67, 69, 82–85, 88, 115, 201n2 (chap. 2)*
  in the kingdom of the Father, *189–192*

reward(s) *(continued)*
  of kingdom of the Son, 60
  for labor(ing in the Father's family business), 54, 59–60, 83–85
  for martyrdom, 22
  of merit, 60
  of new body, 86–92, 131
  for paying the price, 160
  of ruling and reigning with the Lord, 84
  for seeking Him diligently, 190
  for service, 53, 60, 84–85, 131, 180–181, 182
  for sharing in His sufferings, 87
  for work(s), 82–85, 118, 138, 182
Roman Empire, 20–25, 166
Roman Catholic Church, 19–20, 22–25, 156, 166, 172
Roman Catholic Encyclopedia, 19
"Roman Catholicism," 204n5
Romans
  1:1, 201n1 *(chap. 1)*
  1:16, 201n2 *(chap. 1)*
  1:25, 196t
  3:24, 13
  5:21, 13, 195t
  6:6, 8, 73
  6:22, 195t
  6:23, 195t
  8:4, 106
  8:8, 121
  8:14, 116t
  8:17, 61t, 58–59
  8:17–18, 74, 87
  8:18, 49, 59
  8:19, 50
  8:23–24, 185
  9:15, 196t
  11:25, 37, 45
  11:33, 132
  11:36, 196t
  12:2, 195t
  14:10–12, 81
  15:16, 16, 201n1 *(chap. 1)*
  15: 19, 29, 201n2 *(chap. 1)*
  16:25, 44, 157, 196t
  16:26, 195t
  16:27, 196t
Rutz, James, 20, 201n1 *(chap. 2)*

S
Sabbath, 32, 102
sabbatismos, 32, 102–103
salvation, 9, 183–186
  of body, 185
  of grace, 55
  of soul, 16, 61t, 184–185
  of spirit, 16, 61t, 183–184, 185
Semiramis, 165, 168
sheowl, 134
Sides, Dale M., 203n1 *(chap. 15)*, 203n1 *(chap. 16)*, 204n2
Sides, Vicki, 204n1
skopeo, 89–90
skotos, 128
sole fide, 171–172
song, 71. *See also* hymn
Song of Solomon (book), 63
sozo, 183
stasis, 87
Stone Upon Stone: Psalms of Remembrance, 81
Strong's Exhaustive Concordance of the Bible, 102, 183
sun, 131
suffering(s), 49, 116t. *See also* sufferings and glory of the Lord
  joint-heirs and, 59, 74, 87
  of Paul, 87–88
sufferings and glory of the Lord, 41–50, 160–161
syncretism, 22, 166

T
talent(s), 94–98
teeth, gnashing of, 3, 91, 123–125, 126t, 133
teknon, 59–60
1 Thessalonians
  2:2, 8–9, 201n1 *(chap. 1)*
  2:19, 84
  3:2, 201n2 *(chap. 1)*
  4:16–17, 37, 38
  4:17, 130–131
2 Thessalonians
  1:9, 195t
  2:7, 37, 46
  2:16, 195t

INDEX

time out, 130, 132, 133, 141, 152
1 Timothy
  1:16, 195t
  1:17, 196t
  6:12, 195t
  6:16, 195t
  6:17, 195t
  6:19, 195t
2 Timothy
  1:9, 196t
  2 (chapter), 71
  2:5, 14, 111
  2:10, 195t
  2:11–13, 71, 73, 152
  2:12, 49, 74
  2:13, 73, 74
  4:1, 129, 178
  4:6–8, 114
  4:8, 84
  4:10, 195t
  4:18, 196t
Titus
  1:2, 74, 195t
  2:12, 195t
  3:4–7, 55, 183–184
  3:7, 13, 61t, 196t
tribulation, 39, 116t. *See also* great tribulation
triple indemnity, 189

V

Venus, 165, 166, 168

W

wedding garment, 38, 116t
  parable of Matthew 22 and, 65–66
  marriage supper of the Lamb and, 67
week of millennia, 30–33, 102, 202n2 (chap. 3)
weeping 64, 91, 123–125, 126t
Witness of the Stars, 202n1 (chap. 5), 202n1 (chap. 7)
Woodrow, Ralph, 203n1 (app. A), 203n3, 203n4

Y

Yahweh, 176–177

Yahweh—The Sacred Name of God, 204n1
"Your Life Is a Book," 81–82

Z

Zechariah
  6:12–13, 188t
  9:10, 188t
  14:1–4, 34
  14:4, 42
  14:14, 188t
Zondervan Encyclopedia of the Bible, 203n2

THE GOSPEL OF THE KINGDOM TAUGHT LIVE

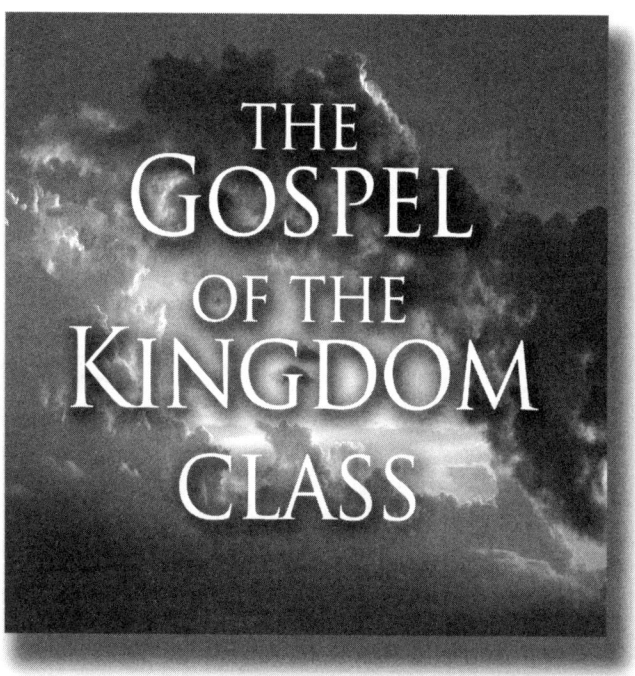

LIVE CLASSES: The truths covered in *The 1,000 Year Reign of Jesus Christ on the Earth* are available by live presentation for groups of all kinds. Gospel of the Kingdom classes are presented throughout the United States and overseas, making a positive impact on churches, cities, and individuals. Many life-changing decisions are made during these classes. To schedule *your* class, contact Liberating Ministries for Christ International, Inc. (LMCI).

DVD OR CD SETS: The DVD class is designed to cross reference the material contained within this book and includes workbooks for study groups. The CD class contains a syllabus designed for small group study as well as individual.

For more information, contact: Liberating Ministries for Christ Int'l.
PO Box 38 ❖ Bedford, VA 24523 ❖ Phone 540-586-5813
Fax 540-586-9372 ❖ www.LMCI.org

BOOKS AND BOOKLETS
BY DALE M. SIDES

40 Days of Communion in Your Home

Angels in the Army: How to Release the Heavenly Host in Sprital Warfare

Approved of God—by Grace or by Works?

Devil, Give Me Back My Money!

Diverse Kinds of Tongues

Flowing in All Nine Gifts of the Holy Spirit

God Damn Satan: Subduing the Evil Kingdom through the Power of Biblical Cursing

Mending Cracks in the Soul

Closing Gates of Hell

Perfect Redemption: The Purpose of His Passion

The Anointing In and On

The Ministry of Liberality

The Three Doctrines of Damnation

True Confessions of Spiritual Warriors

Understanding and Breaking the Schemes of the Devil

Utilizing Gift Ministries

You Don't Have to Be Smart to Walk with God

For more information, contact:
Liberating Ministries for Christ Int'l ❖ PO Box 38 ❖ Bedford, VA 24523
540-586-5813 ❖ Fax 540-586-9372 ❖ www.LMCI.org

PERFECT REDEMPTION: THE PURPOSE OF HIS PASSION

by Dale M. Sides

Most Christians know more about the blood of Jesus through songs we have sung and movies we have seen, than through the Bible we have read. Isn't it time to take a closer look for ourselves? Jesus Christ suffered for a reason—to redeem us. He bled seven different ways to free us from bondage, break off curses, and empower us for a life of victory. Learn the purpose of His passion. Discover your rights—Jesus paid for them with His own blood. Claim your perfect redemption.

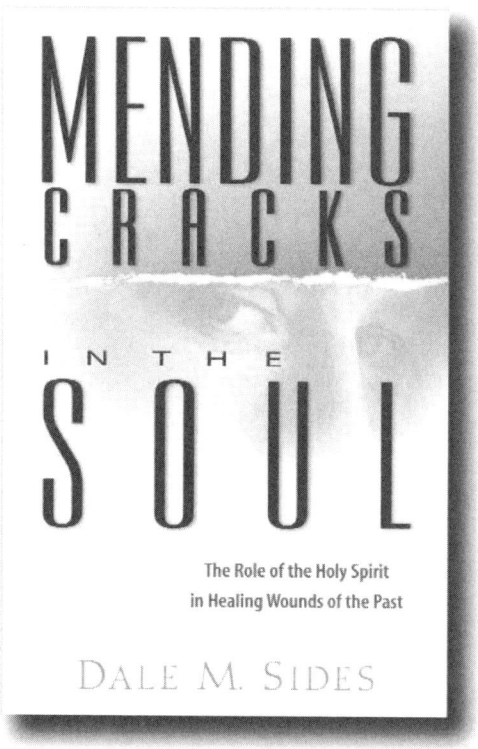

MENDING CRACKS IN THE SOUL

by Dale M. Sides

This powerful and delivering book covers the subject of memory healing through the ministry of the Holy Spirit. Strongly grounded in biblical documentation and practical experience, Dale teaches how a soul can crack due to trauma, how the Holy Spirit can reveal the truth, and how that crack can be forever mended. This book is an invaluable resource to those seeking freedom from the past and to those who minister healing.

DEVIL, GIVE ME BACK MY MONEY!

by Dale M. Sides

This booklet disarms the deception of the devil about money. It reveals that money is spiritual and necessary to fulfill your ministry. Dale M. Sides gives practical instruction from the Word of God on how to take back your money from the devil by proclamation of authority. Thousands of people have been financially liberated by applying these truths in their lives.

ANGELS IN THE ARMY:
HOW TO RELEASE THE HEAVENLY HOST IN SPIRITUAL WARFARE

by Dale M. Sides

This book discloses new information from the Dead Sea Scrolls that verifies age-old principles from the Bible—that mankind has been given the authority to release angels into spiritual warfare. Learn how to be a part of the Lord's army and work with the heavenly host to bring the will of God upon the earth.

God Damn Satan:
Subduing the Evil Kingdom through the Power of Biblical Cursing

by Dale M. Sides

The curse is a major, powerful tool in the Christian's arsenal to use against God's archenemy. Learn how Satan stole this weapon and how you can reclaim it in order to subdue the evil spirit realm.

PO Box 974
Bedford, VA 24523-0974
540-586-2622 Phone
540-586-9372 Fax
www.liberatingpublications.com

ORDER FORM

Qty.	Description	Price	Ext. Price
	Subtotal		
	Sales Tax*		
	Shipping & Handling		
	Total Order		

*Virginia residents add 5% sales tax.

Standard Shipping & Handling Rates	
Orders under $25.00	Add $3.95
Orders $25.01 – $75.00	Add $5.95
Orders over $75.00	Add $7.95

(Please call for expedited delivery rates.)

Name _____

Address _____

City, State, ZIP _____

Daytime Phone _____

Payment   ___Check   ___VISA   ___Master Card

Card # _____ Exp. _____

Signature _____